PORNOGRAPHY
The Sexual Mirage

PORNOGRAPHY
The Sexual Mirage

15703

John W. Drakeford
and
Jack Hamm

Thomas Nelson Inc.
Nashville / New York

Library of Congress Cataloging in Publication Data

Drakeford, John W.
  Pornography: the Sexual Mirage.

  Includes bibliographical references.
  1. Literature, Immoral.   2. Art, Immoral.
  3. Obscenity (Law)—United States. I. Hamm, Jack, joint author.
  II. Title.
HQ471.D7   176'.8   73-7599
  ISBN 0-8407-5051-X

For

ROBINA AND DORISNEL

our wives who have patiently put up with husbands
spending long hours with abhorrent material and as
partners and lovers have contrasted vividly with the
mindless portrayals of pornographic femininity.

PORNOGRAPHY
The Sexual Mirage

PREFACE

I confess at the outset I was lukewarm about this book. My time was taken with teaching, writing, counseling, and conducting conferences. Writing offered increasingly exciting possibilities and I had plans for two new projects. I often ran across mild pornography, but for me it was a mild irritant and I had some sort of vague idea that if I ignored it it would go away.

Then came Jack Hamm. This remarkable artist, author of fourteen books on art, and laden with honors, had not hesitated to champion unpopular causes using his artistic ability to draw cartoons that carried hard-hitting messages in newspapers across the land.

Jack's artistic spirit had been repelled by the inroads of pornography, particularly in demeaning art, and also in literature and movies. Moreover, as a family man and the father of four children, two boys and two girls, he was concerned about what pornography might be doing to family life and the rising generation.

Jack Hamm became a crusader. He launched himself into an in-depth investigation which lasted for three years during which time he amassed a tremendous collection of some 3,000 items. He rapidly became an authority on pornography in America.

Jack's simple thesis—people do not violently oppose pornography because they are ignorant as to its true nature. Few have the time or inclination to take a good close look at these materials and consequently don't know what it is really all about.

After a telephone conversation in which I undertook to consider collaboration, Jack Hamm arrived at my office with large boxes of files, newspapers, hard and soft core magazines, posters, and every conceivable form of pornography. The collection dealt me such a shock that I immediately made plans to remove it from my office, to my private study lest students should get an idea that their professor had become either a compulsive purchaser or a marketer of smut.

I decided to take up the challenge.

Not only had Jack Hamm done all this research but he continued to actively feed material and new information to me. A day without a communication from him seemed strangely incomplete, and my telephone bill reached a new series of highs. So all the basic research and leg work have been done by Jack Hamm.

However, the writing is mine. We agreed that multiple writers make for a patchwork product. From all of the material provided by Jack Hamm I selected what I considered appropriate and in some instances added some of my own. Jack accepted my judgment.

For this book I accept responsibility.

As a practicing psychologist, concerned to a large extent with marriage and family counseling, I am asking for a long cool look at the whole problem of pornography.

JOHN W. DRAKEFORD

CONTENTS

Chapter One

The Underground Literature

The man's appearance gave no indication of his purpose. His smartly cut business suit indicated Brooke's Brothers, and the carefully knotted tie at his throat bespoke good taste, the attache case in hand obviously gave the appearance of containing important documents.

He looked alertly from side to side as he hurried along the sidewalk giving the impression that he was a man with a mission. Apprehensive thoughts chased through his mind—what if after all this trouble he couldn't find it? He quickly dismissed the idea—he must keep a positive attitude.

Arriving at the first newsstand he went into action with enthusiasm and determination. His experienced eye swept rapidly across the plethora of literature on display. Periodically he set down his case, picked up a publication, and ran his eyes down the table of contents; in some instances he flipped over the pages casting rapid glances at the illustrations.

All in vain. Not a copy anywhere.

He'd have to take a risk—steel himself against ridicule. He moved towards the man at the cash register, waited while he made the change for a customer. Happily the concessionaire turned a friendly face toward him. Though he hated doing it, he leaned over to whisper in the man's ear.

As if to make sure that he wasn't under surveillance, the newsman glanced quickly around. If word got around that he stocked this type of literature it might hurt his business. Confident that there were no observing eyes, he reached under the counter. He picked up the publication, dropped it into a paper sack, slipped the package into the customer's hand, plucked the money from him, then sent him on his way with a "Don't tell anyone you bought it here" sort of look.

Once home and safely ensconced in his easy chair in front of the crackling fire, the literature shopper propped up his feet and relaxed. It had been a hectic experience, and he was lucky to get it, and he had both a glow of satisfaction and a sense of accomplishment.

He reached over, opened his briefcase, and pulled out the paper sack. With a sigh of contentment he settled down to read his *Time* magazine.

Exaggeration?

Don't be too sure. It might well be that we're close to the day when high quality magazines will be kept under the counter while the shelves will be loaded down with publications that carry only one news item—sex.

A commonly used yardstick by which a country's educational level is measured is the literacy rate. If this rate is high the situation is considered good. So one of the prime concerns of any educational program is to teach people to read. But having taught them the skill, what sort of material will we put in their hands?

If the present trend keeps up, they certainly won't be reading many magazines that will inform their minds and challenge their spirits. Many of the magazines that played such an important role in the past development of America are disappearing. *Colliers,* and *Look,* for example, have all vanished from the newsstands.

News agents and sellers of literature have found new stock for their shelves. The profit margin is higher, the material un-dated so that it never becomes stale, and some enterprising entrepreneurs clip off the printed prices and charge as much as the trade will stand; so the store owner, feeling very righteous in utilizing capitalism's profit motive, fills his shelves with goods that will bring him a greater return.

One Houston bookseller handles all types of literature, in-cluding college textbooks, but readily admits that his greatest profits come from what he frankly refers to as "obscene paper-backs."

Starting from scratch in Southern California, the so-called "Adult Bookstores" were doing a $20 million per year business within two years. Small wonder the entrepreneur has been

THEY ARE INSEPARABLE

"LIBERTY CANNOT BE ESTAB-
LISHED WITHOUT MORALITY,
NOR MORALITY WITHOUT
FAITH." — *HORACE GREELEY*

LIBERTY
MORALITY
FAITH

quick to get in on the burgeoning field.

A professional journal for librarians recently contained a long article on the "pornographic collection" with the suggestion that perhaps the time has come for libraries to provide pornographic material for the general public.

This interest of the library in contemporary materials may be cold comfort for the struggling author who, unable to sell his "square" writings and is on his way to collect his welfare check, stops by the library and is confronted with the acquisitions shelf proudly displaying the "latest erotica."

He can at least console himself that because of his impecunious condition he is unable to pay his taxes and so support the library and its activities of circulating pornography.

Reports come from across the nation, and the average citizen begins to wonder if there is nowhere to go as he feels the pressure from the pornographic triangle of New York on the east and Los Angeles and San Francisco on the west as three great centers belch forth an unending stream of smut that threatens to inundate the nation.

America's largest city, New York, has the dubious honor of having its 42nd Street, long noted for theater, become the most notorious retailing point for pornography; and the development is affecting what for many years was the number one glamour spot of the theater.

As the year 1972 tottered to a close, *Time* magazine (December 25, p. 76) reported that Broadway, the traditional home of the theater, lay in a critical if not mortal condition in which life was at a low ebb, "In all, 16 of Broadway's 34 theaters were dark last week. Of the 18 only a handful . . . were taking in enough at the box office to make a profit for the shows and for themselves."

The article goes on, "What is the cause of the problem? A lack of good plays? The unions? The exodus to the suburbs? The economy? A major factor is the decline of the Times Square-Broadway neighborhood, with its prostitutes, massage parlors and porno emporiums."

Forty-second Street was known as the *Great White Way,* but it may be necessary to change that name. A man robbed a bank and, as he fled down Forty-second Street, two zealous bank employees took out after him. They were risking their lives but they had the reasonable expectation that at two o'clock in the afternoon they could keep track of the man until they encountered a police officer.

After two blocks of pursuit their hopes for assistance from the law began to fade so they overtook and apprehended the hold-up man, a crowd quickly surrounded the struggling trio and help finally arrived—for the hold-up man. The crowd compelled the bank employees·to release the criminal.

Commenting on the incident the *New York Times* January 7,

1972, said, "The region, once celebrated as The Great White Way has virtually been abandoned to sleazy peep shows, petty thieves, pimps, panhandlers, and loiterers in search of the unwary and unprotected."

It's not without the bounds of possibility that the *Great White Way* may become the *Great Red Light Way.*

The editor of one of the cheapest (in content if not in price) sex tabloids has actually come up with a scheme to rejuvenate the unfortunate Square.

Inspired by a city in Germany that has built an "Eros Center", the plan calls for the Square to be completely blocked off and surrounded by a wall that will keep out children, with admissions through turnstiles into which each of the visitors would be required to deposit fifty cents. Within, prostitutes would peddle their wares. Because of the absence of pimps, the girls would be fairly taxed on their earnings. Social centers would abound: homosexual theaters, lesbian theaters, gay bars, swingers' bars, singles' bars, and sex stores offering all sorts of exotic sexual wares.

Shades of Sodom and Gommorah!!!

This shocking situation in the nation's largest city may be indicative of the monumental pornography problem faced by our country today.

But even as we use such words as "pornography" we are confronted with semantic problems of tremendous proportions. As the grand old man in the use of four-letter words, novelist Henry Miller, has said, "To discuss the nature and meaning of pornography is almost as difficult as it is to talk about God."

Definitions abound.

A sexologist, "Pornography is material deliberately designed to produce strong sexual arousal."

Or more graphically in the words of D. H. Lawrence, "Doing dirt on sex."

And the more informal descriptions.

"Pornography is actually a form of prostitution because it advertises and advocates sex for sale, pleasure for a price."

"Pornography is masturbation—meant to arouse sexual interest in the absence of personal human contact let alone a one-to-one human relationship."

But above everything else, pornography is the sexual mirage. By its very nature a mirage lives in the individual's mind. In the case of a weary traveler, his thirst fosters the image of an oasis with springs of water, verdant pasture, palm trees, and the promise of everything the traveler needs. But it has no reality. As fast as the traveler approaches, just that fast his mirage retreats from him. This is exactly the nature of pornography. It is fiction removed from the world of fact.

In this volume we will focus on the phantasmagoria of pornography, its varied forms, techniques, media, the activities it promotes, the amazing investigation by a presidential commission, the arguments for pornography and their answer, the legal mess, the indictment against pornography, and finally a plan of action for meeting the situation.

A 'NEW' WORSHIP

Chapter Two

A Bunny Blanket
Became A Sex Philosophy

The dramatic two-page spread depicts a man making a desperate effort to prevent himself falling over the edge and into the yawning chasm below. One leg dangles down behind him; hands stretched out above him claw for a precarious hold while the knee of his other leg has fortuitously found a projection into which it snugly fits, providing him with a modicum of security.

Closer inspection shows that the projection that offers a knee hold is, of all things, the nipple of an enormous female breast.

The spread is contained in an issue of *Playboy* magazine, and must have some peculiar symbolic meaning for a publication that has spent its years of existence majoring on the female breast. Despite the put-down of that other prophet of the sexual world, David Reubens, who says the female breast is nothing more than a large sweat gland, the publishers of *Playboy* have maintained and fostered a concern with, and worship of, what one woman calls "improbable mammary glands."

This emphasis has certainly paid off for the publisher and he has milked an enormous fortune from these improbable oversized breasts. It has been estimated that Hugh Hefner's net worth currently stands somewhere around the $168 million mark, give or take a million or two.

Perhaps in an effort to show what a high flyer he has really become, in 1970 Hefner made the plunge and bought himself the ultimate status symbol in transportation—a Douglas DC9-30 airplane. The plane, which in normal airline use accommodates one hundred five passengers, was built into a custom configura-

17

tion to transport 38 people sitting or 16 lying down. Painted black, it has the white rabbit emblem of the Playboy world on the tail, painted in such a position that it can be illuminated at night by search lights located on the rear tips of the wings.

The interior of the black bird is as ornate and spectacular as the exterior dark and sinister, containing amongst other things a living room-discotheque, a card room, and bedroom, which to begin with had a huge elliptical bed covered with Tasmanian possum skins. Two movie projectors, seven TV monitors, video apparatus, and a movie screen raised and lowered by buttons help to make it more livable.

In addition to all these mechanical devices the aircraft has eight stewardesses, known of course as "bunnies." These girls were specially chosen from 800 "bunnies" already working at Playboy clubs. They were given a special twenty-seven day training which included first aid, preparing food, grooming, and naturally, mouth-to-mouth resuscitation.

Hefner refers to the plane as his "black mother in the sky." Apparently he desperately needs mother's protection, because, prior to this plunge into the transportation business, he lived away in his windowless mansion, built in this manner no doubt to frustrate the activities of peeping toms. On his first trip to Europe he became so fearful and nervous that after only one short week he abandoned his venture and fled back to the protection of his windowless castle in Chicago. Hefner commented on the episode, "Call it womb sickness."

He has come a long way since that December day in 1953 when he launched his new magazine. He had learned the lesson of publishers of questionable literature and put no date on the cover of the new publication. Using this little trick, he knew that if the magazine didn't sell, he'd be able to leave them on the stands for an indefinite period in the hope that they'd finally find some takers.

But he needn't have worried. He'd developed a formula of displaying female flesh that would titillate masculine sexuality. Marilyn Monroe led off as being the first naked "sweetheart," and shortly afterwards he introduced the "Playmate of the Month" for voyeuristic American males.

Estimates of *Playboy*'s circulation vary, but one of the most recent put it at 5,908,173 copies per month. The public relations department of the magazine claims newsstand sales bring the figure to 11,000,000. They further claim that each issue is read by seven people, bringing the grand total to some 77,000,000 pairs of eyes.

And what do all these eyes see?

Very little of the printed text, apparently.

In a conference of writers who contributed to the magazine, Nicholas von Hoffman remarked, "How can anybody critique this magazine which nobody reads? I couldn't read my own piece. I read the first page and then—boob alley!—(vernacular for busts) I was lost in the boobs."[1]

It has been estimated that if all the Playmates who have appeared in the centerfold of *Playboy* magazine were transformed into one girl, she would weigh eleven and a half tons and have a bust of 7,242 inches, with this latter figure of much more importance than the former.

Commenting on this fact, Hefner unequivocally states his position, "Well, big breasts are part of human sexuality. Now we have been running a *few* smaller breasts—a couple of months ago we ran a girl who was little more than boy—but throughout history breasts have been major erotic symbols. And the publisher happens to like them."[2]

Perhaps the clue to *Playboy* magazine may be to follow the lead of many of its alleged readers who apparently do little reading of the long dull paragraphs of the text and focus on the illustrations.

One of *Playboy*'s lesser cartoons shows a naked male opening the door of a closet where a row of nude women are hanging upside down with knees bent from a rail. The male stands and looks them over as if he were selecting what tie, shoes, or suit he would wear today. Women are available, limp, inert, and unresisting, so that the all-powerful male can make his choice.

Hefner is high on civil liberties. But he insists on certain limitations on some people's freedom—particularly those . . . er . . . women.

Looking around for windmills to fight, this Don Quixote of sexual freedom decided that the Women's Lib might offer some pleasing fare for his readers. He even went as far as to commission a woman for the sum of $2,000 to write an article on Women's Lib. Apparently the piece was at first acceptable, even though the authoress referred to the Masters and Johnson

conclusion that women can have more intense orgasms by masturbating than by sleeping with men which didn't fit in with
Playboy philosophy.

But about this time disquieting news came filtering through
to Hefner's ears. His intelligence forces, ever alert for new
developments in the world of men-women relationships, reported that Women's Lib and *Playboy* mightn't really be bed-
mates. It seems that the rank and file of women's libers took a
dim view of *Playboy* and actually had the effrontry to mount an
anti-Playboy campaign. Overwhelmed by the crass ingratitude
of the sex that owed so much to him, in a shocking un-liberal
move, the irritated editor quietly killed the article by the
women's lib sympathizer and employed a well-known writer to
pen a piece entitled, "Up Against the Wall Male Chauvinist
Pig." In this the author let go a blast of invectives at the
women's libers and predictably relegated them to "the discard
file of history."

Appalled by all this talk of feminine freedom and women
demanding rights was too much for Hefner, and he dictated an
inter-office memo to his editorial director.

*"These chicks are our natural enemy . . . It is time to do battle with
them . . . What I want is a devastating piece that takes the militant
feminists apart. [They are] unalterably opposed to the romantic boy-
girl society that Playboy promotes . . . Let's get to it and let's make it
a real winner."*[3]

The *Playboy* equivalent of *Advice to the Lovelorn* goes under
the name of *The Playboy Advisor*. Here readers are invited to
submit "all reasonable questions—from fashion, food, and
drink, stereo and sports cars, to dating dilemmas, taste and
etiquette."

Although there are letters inquiring about how to buy a car
in Europe and what to do about a stereo that's making strange
noises and the best way to look after your shoes, the column is
laced with questions about sex with replies that conform to the
Playboy philosophy.

One wife writes to tell of her husband who had very limited
sexual experiences before their marriage, he only slept with
one other person. She suspects he would like to copulate with
other women. As far as she is concerned that's okay, she's
broadminded but she has a lurking fear that after he's had

these experiences with another woman he may become emotionally involved with his new partner.

Answer: If you think you'll enjoy it without guilt or jealousy then forget the rationalization about your husband possibly becoming involved with someone else.

A serviceman writes to tell that when he was going to Vietnam he took the enlightened position that his wife needed sexual expression while he was away, and he told her that if she wanted to have sex with someone else—just go ahead. His wife was upset by the suggestion, but after he'd been away for a year she had a brief affair and went to bed with another man. Feeling guilty, his wife wrote her absent spouse and admitted she followed his original suggestion. Now he was resentful.

Answer: Your wife should not have told you about the experience.

A letter from a twenty-four-year-older tells about his relationship with his girlfriend, age twenty-one. The young lady wants to come to marriage a virgin, but he is vividly aware of a pressing sexual desire. He says, "Should I press the sexual issue to the hilt, if you'll pardon the expression."

Answer: You should have a frank talk with your girl about the dubious advantages of walking down the aisle as a virgin—with a nervous wreck at her side.

A companion feature in *Playboy* is the Playboy Forum titled as "an interchange of ideas between reader and editor on subjects raised by 'the Playboy philosophy.' "

This section embraces a wide variety of subjects and occasionally brings to light some sensible discussion, that is by the writer, not by the answerer. One such letter reads:

I have never objected to Playboy, *because, by and large, I have found that the magazine and* The Playboy Philosophy *are reasonable. But today, as I read all the letters, the news reports, the Mae West interview and the many jokes, advertisements, cartoons, stories and articles in a recent issue, one strong thought exploded in my mind, grew and became terribly insistent.*

As I read of abortion and vasectomy, unwed mothers and homes for unwanted children, homosexuals, protestors and syphilis, I kept wondering. "Why, in the name of God and common sense, does not a magazine with the power of Playboy *use the word chastity every now and again and explain, explore and expound to the fullest the merits, virtues and, yea, even the plain, old-fashioned convenience of chaste*

*living? Why does everybody seem to think they can go about the world
fornicating rampantly without paying a heavy price, whether they be
male or female, bond or free?"*

*The human body doesn't need sexual intercourse to be healthy and
happy. Sex just isn't that important and it should not be. The act of
physical sex unprotected from illegitimate procreation does not spell
love. It spells madness.*

*Along with anti-pollution, please, can't we preach chastity at least
as loudly as we preach abortion?*

Mrs.
Illinois

To such a thoughtful epistle, Playboy has a one line put-
down: "Chaste makes waste."

It is almost an act of poetic justice that the publisher of
Playboy who has the sorriest view of womanhood, should suf-
fer his most devastating put-down at the hands of a woman.
Gloria Steinem, the attractive, aggressive journalist and
women's liber, visited Hefner in his Chicago mansion where, in
contrast to his openness in displaying aspects of human sexuality, he hides himself away in a windowless retreat.

Naturally enough, this perceptive woman's eyes lighted on
the Bunny dormitory which houses girls from the local Playboy
club. Here they pay rent and hang their belongings in wooden
lockers that reminded the observer of some long ago high
school.

When Steinem talked with Hefner about the status of women
and astounded him with the news that a number of women in
his colony were dissatisfied with their lot in life, he looked hurt
at their gross ingratitude and made plain he was almost a
women's liber himself. He declared himself to be in favor of
females being able to vote, own property, etc., but he wanted
them preeminently ". . . to be attractive to men." He then
added about the women in his own enterprises, "I think I
know what they want and what makes them happy."

Steinem's response was classic, "You sound like a good-
hearted plantation owner who's deeply hurt when his slaves
start rebelling."[4]

In many ways this woman has put her finger on what may be
the preeminent problem of *Playboy*—its portrayal of women.

The woman of *Playboy* magazine is a fiction—a figment of
the male mind—a masculine wish fulfillment.

Responding to a question by a reader, Hy Gardner zeroed in on the portrayal of the "Playmate of the Month."

Q: Those Playboy Playmates of the Month. How come they don't have any imperfections? No warts? No scars? No blemishes at all? How do Hefner's people find such perfect specimens?

—*Dean O'R, Las Vegas*

A: The Skin You Love to Touch comes courtesy of the retouch artists at Playboy's printing plant. Here's how it's done. After scanning scores of photographs, the Playmate of the Month's centerfold is chosen. Impeccably air-brushed, the photos get a second go-around when etcher Julius Block (of Chicago's Regenstein Printing Co.) removes all remaining distractions. Including any appendix or other scars and wrinkles. Freckles either stay on or come off—depending on the diagnosis of dermatologist Hefner. [5]

These physically perfect masculine wish-fulfillment women are part of what some observers see as Hefner's blatant pitch to his special market. A full page statement aimed at enlisting more advertisers claims that *Playboy* is read by three out of four males in college and one out of every two men under 35 in professional and managerial occupations. The ad wooing the advertisers proclaims, "If you want to get to the top of the market, put your message where men are on the move up—in *Playboy.*"

The great message is that there are certain things in life that no up-and-coming young man should be without. Clothes, automobile, liquor, and girls—especially girls.

Playboy is sex without any vestige of relationship. One of the cartoons shows an over-endowed nude girl sitting on the edge of the bed she has just shared with the male who with towel draped around him is shaving in the adjoining bathroom. The girl is talking on the telephone and saying, "I think he's getting serious, Mother—he asked me to stay for lunch."

For *Playboy,* women are the personification of lust. They live for nothing as much as to seduce men. These mythical females spend days, and especially nights, searching for opportunities to bid males who will copulate with them. Undoubtedly women are more physiologically suited to orgiastic enterprises than are men. Unlike the male they can participate in coitus whether they have desire or not, with the erective factor of no importance to them.

But psychologically—that's another matter.

By the very nature of human sexuality, and the physiological factors involved, man is the aggressor to the act and feminine sexuality much more a response to these overtures. *Playboy*'s efforts to make every woman the personification of female lust forever spending her days on a quest for males who can be seduced is patently false.

There is considerable evidence about the damage of the hedonistic practices advocated by Hefner.

Dr. O. Hobart Mowrer, research psychologist at the University of Illinois says, "In essence Freudian theory holds that anxiety comes from evil wishes, from acts which the individual would commit if he dared. The alternative view here proposed is that anxiety comes, not from acts which the individual would commit but dares not, but from acts which he *has committed,* but wishes that he had not. It is, in other words, a "guilt theory" of anxiety rather than an "impulse theory."[6]

Effectiveness of this form of therapy which in some instances being nearly miraculous and is verifiable by some very thorough research work being carried out is a refutation of the idea that unlimited sexual expression is universal cure-all for any sort of mental difficulties.

In one of its most arrogant assertions, *Playboy* claims to have 3,000,000 women readers. If there is any basis in fact for this assertion, some of the female readers might take note of Gloria Steinem who said in response to Hefner's assertion that he wanted women to be attractive to men, "Well I want men to be attractive to women. But I don't want their whole identity to rest on that. There are times when a woman reading *Playboy* feels a little like a Jew reading a Nazi manual."[7]

One of the great problems we face today is a desensitizing of our finest susceptibilities turning us into what one writer has called, " . . . a nation of 200 million involuntary peeping toms."

He goes on to say, "*Playboy* is the proto-villain in all of this, the first mass pusher of the drug of sex to the sensually disadvantaged of all ages, the first mass marketer of measured doses of addictive sexual sensation."[8]

The tragedy of all this is that if an individual takes the Playboy Philosophy as a guide for life, he is leaning on a broken reed. This philosophy has no place for marriage. The all-important consideration is that a person can never get enough sex and no single partner will ever satisfy his surging lust. As for the family?

What of religion and *Playboy*?

The Publisher likes nothing more than to get some ministers involved in propagating his philosophy, and many of the hireling prophets being what they are, fall for the *Playboy* line.

Playboy really has a big time flogging the dead horse of Puritanism. Puritanism is to blame for every evil that humans face. Hefner likes to speak in lofty terms of the battle that he has carried on against the Protestant ethic. This Protestant ethic he equates with conservatism and what he speaks of as the "right." He claims this conservatism is anti-racial, anti-social, and anti-sexual.

In his strange mixed-up thinking he sees the Protestant ethic as opposed to capitalism. During an interview when he was asked about his positions he said, "I don't think possessions are bad. I'm not ashamed of them. That hangup is part of the Protestant ethic."

He sounds rather like the parrot who is constantly repeating the same worn-out phrase without knowing what it means, and overlooks the fact that many authorities in the field believe that the Protestant ethic was an important factor in the development of capitalism. With the rise of Protestantism people saw their work as their calling, their religious commitment meant they lived austere lives and didn't spend much money, so accumulation followed. Hefner, in his ignorance, completely overlooks the relationship of Protestantism and Capitalism.

Another interesting aspect of the attitude of Hefner to the Protestant ethic was brought to light by Gloria Steinem in her interview with *Playboy*'s owner.

Hefner: "I don't know who my enemies are, but I suspect they've a lot more than that (the post office). All those people who believe in the Protestant Ethic and who . . ."

"Buy your magazine," Steinem interjected, "sexual frustration is certainly a major factor in getting people to buy *Playboy*. In a way you're weakening your learning from it. Where would you be without the Protestant Ethic?"

At this point Hefner diverted the discussion to justify his wealth.

Of course Hefner will use ministers and priests when it suits him. In one issue of *Playboy* he ran a full page spread on abortion. This man who has done so much to degrade the image of woman now emerges as their champion and puts in a subheading, " . . . the holy war to protect the 'right to life' of the fetus gets into high gear—and American women are the victims."

The listings that follow tell of the location and telephone numbers of *Clergy Consultation Services* which will help put pregnant girls in touch with abortion services.

But basically Hefner is hostile to religion, and Elton Trueblood, the eminent philosopher, suspects that the whole *Playboy* phenomenon may be establishing a new religion which he sees as, "a genuine rival to Christianity."

Apparently Hefner has some pretty heady views about himself that may not be opposed to this notion. In an interview he stated, "I would rather be me than, say, Richard Burton. Whatever I am is unique. I'm sure that I'll be remembered as one significant part of our time. We are living in a period of rapid sociological change and I am on the side of angels." Angels . . . or devils?

That might just be one of the reasons why he bought the giant airplane that *Time* magazine referred to as the flying womb.

A womb is necessary for birth and many psychologists have taken note of people who apparently live in the memory of a sheltered interuterine existence of the long, long ago and spend all their days in a feverish attempt to "return to the womb," rather than moving on towards new heights of development and achievement that are sometimes referred to as the *maturing* processes.

In one of his few moments of candor, Hefner, asked why he had made such a big deal about rabbits—bunnies—answered, "I suppose the Freudians would try to make something out of this. When I was a little boy I had a blanket, a sort of security thing, and I called it my bunny blanket."

Bless his little cotton-tailed heart. No wonder they are called playmates. The little fellow is trying to get away from his security blanket so he can go out and romp around with his playmates.

One of the most illuminating interviews reported in *Playboy* magazine took place with Julius Feiffer, the author of *Carnal*

Knowledge. At the conclusion of the discussion, Feiffer is reminded about the nostalgia fad and he says, "It's my generation's admission that nothing works anymore, so we want out. God died in the early sixties, then the two Kennedys and King, and the electoral process, then somewhere in the middle of all that the family."

"One can already see the signs, intellectuals in despair, parents in despair, hard hats in despair, middle America in confusion, which is their version of despair."

The problem with the philosophy of "eat, drink, and be merry for tomorrow we die" is that we don't die tomorrow. We live with the results of our foolishness.

If the family dies there will be one man who played a definite role—Hefner.

And to cap it all, the one man, more than others, who has separated sex from love said in an interview, "You know in the next ten years I would rather meet a girl and fall in love than make another hundred million dollars."

Chapter Three

The Plot Sickens

The moment the subject of pornography is introduced, one member of the group is bound to speak up and say, "If we start clamping down on pornography, we'll certainly have to clean out the art galleries and the libraries. Why many of the works now recognized as classics could easily be condemned as pornography by some smut crusader."

This attitude is typical of much of the confusion that surrounds any discussion of pornography and fails to distinguish some fundamental differences between hard-core pornography and legitimate literature dealing with the field of human sexuality.

In the non-fiction field publications like marriage manuals realistically portray human sexual experiences. The legitimate books in this field have one element in common—they deal with reality. The reality may be psychological, sociological, or medical in nature, but it is the key to the sexual portrayals of these works.

Even works of fiction, despite the fact that they are the product of the writer's imagination contain an element of reality. This reality is somewhat less tangible than in the non-fiction publications and lies in the effort of the author to communicate the intra-psychic and inter-personal experiences of people in their sexual encounters that take place as an integral part of a plausible story.

The main difference between pornography and these other types of writing is that pornography is not really concerned about reality at all. It is a psychological aphrodisiac which uses literary techniques for evoking erotic imagery to bring about sexual arousal in the mind of its readers. In most of these writings, the plot and its development is in some instances cursory and incidental, and in others conspicuous by its absence.

Pornographic books have been around for a long time, but the year 1969 proved to be a watershed for the marketeers of this type of material. Prior to this time literary presentations of sexuality were somewhat restrained. But court decisions concerning some of the so-called classical pornographic books like *Tropic of Cancer* and *Fanny Hill* gave a signal to publishers that a new era of permissiveness was in the offing, and they were not slow to move in and take advantage of the situation.

In their search for products, publishers looked in the first instance to the so-called "classic" erotic writings in English. When this supply was exhausted, they turned their eyes to foreign erotic writings which were translated and printed. Then, as this source was used up, hack writers standing by moved in to supply the material needed by these suppliers to the burgeoning market.

From 1969 onward publishers were convinced they could publish any type of book with impunity from legal action. As a result of this, a flood of pornography was released, and it has been estimated that in a two to three year period "tens of millions of paperbacks have been sold in the United States which could not possibly be exceeded in candor, graphic description of sexual activity or the use of vulgar language."

The skill of the pornographer who works with such diligence to supply material for the new market lies in three areas: his descriptive powers, his sense of timing, and the development of a theme or themes.

You can be sure that the pornographer's capacity to describe is not just employed on the landscape, architectural masterpieces, or even in portraying the total appearance and personality of individuals. His descriptions are narrowed down to the human body with an almost total focus on the detail—the minute detail—of primary and secondary sexual organs and their functions.

While many pieces of pornography demonstrate no more literary ability than the capacity to string together a series of minutely descriptive erotic scenes, the more successful use a timing technique comparable to that of the skillful mystery writer, with the notable difference that, instead of developing a question as to the identity of the murderer or victim, the pornographer majors on building up sexual tension. He starts with milder sexual scenes and moves through a series of stages in which the erotic imagery is heightened as the characters engage in an ever-widening variety of increasingly unorthodox sexual activities.

The third aspect of pornography is the themes it utilizes. These include defloration, incest, debasement of the religious, the use of gutter language, porno-violence, super-sexed males, seductive females, bestiality, detailed description of sex organs, and eroticising legitimate sex research.

Defloration

Because virginity represents an attitude of mind which is the complete opposite of all that the pornographer's work is based on, the surrender of maidenhood presents an event that to the pornographer might be analogous to a conquering army capturing the capital city of the enemy country. So the act of defloration or deprivation of virginity is portrayed as a high-water mark sexual experience.

The picture is generally painted of a female, who because of a misguided and unenlightened education, or lack of opportunity, has maintained a stance of chastity and so missed the delights of uninhibited sex.

A widely used gimmick is to tell the story of the country girl who has come to the big city. She lives in a house where by chance she peeps through a knot hole in the wall and witnesses two people copulating in the next room. She is amazed by all the physical aspects of male and female genitalia, which are described in the greatest of detail, and as she witnesses the scene, she becomes aware of an overpowering desire to taste of all these sexual delights. She determines to seek the earliest opportunity to find a male—any male—to whom she can offer her virginity in a painful, bloody, but joyous surrender.

Defloration is seen as so important that when one of the heroines goes to work in a house of prostitution she is taught the art of passing herself off as a virgin. She develops a method by which she deceives the customer who is greatly taken with the notion of deflowering an innocent virgin and pays a goodly sum of money to become the victim of this deception.

After the act of violation there may be just a few twinges of conscience, but these are easily put down as the girl in question recalls the tremendous pleasure that has been hers and how grateful she should be to the male who performed this service for her.

This completely false notion that the chaste girl will be a sexual drop-out is not supported by the experiences of many marriage counselors who find that wide premarital sexual experiences may actually prove a hindrance to adjustment in maturer years. The girl with a legacy of promiscuity may finish up with an overlay of guilt if not a more tangible, physical evidence of her sexual deviance.

Incest

One element of pornography is the idea of upsetting normally held taboos on human sexuality. The incest taboo is the most widely held of all sexual prohibitions and offers a tremendous potential to the pornographer as a means of providing sexual stimulation.

In one situation the seductive stepmother carefully sets the scene. She is not much older than her stepson but has been noticing his sexual development. She sees his crude advances to girls and the awareness of the youth's growing sexuality stirs a strange desire within her. She inwardly reasons that she might be able to save him from some of the trouble bound to come from his bumbling approaches and at the same time satisfy her own sex urges.

The resourceful woman carefully prepares her trap by asking the strapping lad to help her with a stuck zipper. Then with a series of carefully planned moves carried out with the skill of a ballerina she maneuvers the awkward boy into a sexual situation and proceeds to skillfully initiate him into sexual activity that leads to a stepmother-son orgy.

Even more prevalent is the theme of the father who seduces or is seduced by his daughter. A variation of the incest theme is the story of a father who visits his little daughter's bed nightly and she in turn indicates her delighted reaction as he initiates her into sexual experiences. Then comes the time when her cousin comes to spend the night. The girls fall into exchanging confidences, and the cousin reveals she is still a virgin. When Pa makes his nightly visit he deflowers his niece,

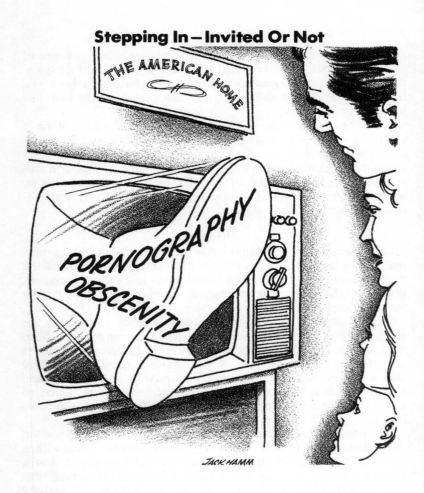

aided and abetted by his daughter with sundry cries of exclamations and delight.

An added flavoring to this scene is brought about by the appearance of the mother, who awakened by the noise comes and stands in the doorway to applaud her husband in his sex orgy with his daughter and niece.

The family angle comes into the picture. A typical story tells of a young man being attracted to the girl and visiting in her home. After a sexual encounter, he finds a similar opportunity of relations with her mother. He soon discovers that her brother and sister are cohabiting, and being invited to become an integral part of the family, he decides to throw in his lot with this group in which all the members of the family share their sexual favors with each other.

Despite the aphrodisiac it provides for readers of pornography, the plain facts of incest are really not pretty. Girls are generally the victims, and, even if they have a certain sense of satisfaction of being able to manipulate Daddy, as life progresses it gives rise to a multiplicity of complications, particularly as they watch their own developing daughters and see them as temptations to their husbands. Having worked for many years in therapy groups, I am vividly aware of the horrible aftermath of incestuous father-daughter relationships and the misery they can bring in later years. There are some compelling reasons why the incest taboo is the most universal of all sexual prohibitions.

Pulitzer Prize winner Howard James, who has made a speciality of studying the subject of children in trouble, has estimated that in America there will be up to one million children who run away from home in any one year. He notes that in most instances, "Sexual abuse is 50 to 100 times more prevalent in producing the battered child that the public has recently become so interested in." He adds, "One-third of girls in detention homes who have been frequent runaways are victims of incest."[1]

Of course, there are serious potential genetic problems. One very broadminded medical man noted that while the Pharaohs of Egypt married within the family, brother and sister, South Sea islanders frowned on incest, sometimes punishing it with death. The writer commented, "Take your choice. The Pharaohs died out, but the primitive islanders lived on."

Debasement of the Religious

Because religion and the church have frequently been the setters of the standards of sexual behavior, one of the tasks of the pornographer is to show that most religionists are really sensualists hiding behind a clerical collar. From the pornography perspective, religion is really an enormous hypocrisy which inflicts unreal standards on the general public while the

Bombardment

religionist lives an underhand life of sexual freedom.

Starting from this basis the pornographer can ward off the monotony which is always his enemy by playing the religious theme with variations.

One popular way to do this is through the use of the Catholic confessional. The idea of people going into a booth and leveling about all their failures and shortcomings in life provides a Peeping Tom's paradise for the pornographer.

A typical story tells of the promiscuous girl who lives a double life by being a nymphomaniac the biggest proportion of her time, and on occasions devoutly attending the services of the Catholic Church.

She visits the confessional box to make her abject confession, and the priest responds by requesting her to be more specific about the details of her misdemeanors. Pausing but a moment the penitent girl pulls out a list from her handbag and

AS ONE, SO THE OTHER

SEX AND FIRE

IN THEIR PROPER PLACE BENEFIT ALL MANKIND

—*BUT WHEN OUT OF CONTROL....!!*

"AVOID SEXUAL LOOSENESS LIKE THE PLAGUE" I COR. 6:18 (PHIL.TRS.)

JACK HAMM

then pours out a long particularized story of her sexual transgressions.

Instead of absolution the priest takes her to his office where he normally prays over the transgressor, but because of the peculiar difficulties, he may need to exorcise the demons of lust and corruption by the "laying on of hands."

A description of the ensuing sexual activities is spiced with appropriate remarks of the conversation such as the girl's comment that she didn't learn anything like this in parochial school, and the priest's response that the church like everything else is changing.

Appropriately, when the encounter is concluded and the girl is leaving the church, the priest calls out to remind her that she should leave a donation for the building fund.

So the pornographer moves on in the guise as a crusader who is hard at work exposing the hypocrisy of organized religion.

The Use of Gutter Language

Hard core pornography is characterized by one invariable literary method—the use of gutter language.

Language has always presented a dilemma for the pornographer, who prefers non-verbal imagery and would abolish language if he could, but language being the vehicle of literary communication he is astute enough to turn it to his advantage by using gutter language as a means of heightening the erotic effect.

Most parents trying to sexually educate their children become aware that we have no really good offhand neutral terms to refer to human genitals, and most terms fall into one of four categories: nursery terms, archaisms, scientific terms, gutter terms.

All of this may be telling us that men and women need some privacy in life and genitals are sometimes referred to as "private parts." Unlike animals, most humans have a sense of shame when their genitals are exposed. Even among the most uninhibited primitive tribes the tendency remains for people to hide their genitals from prying eyes.

The favorite scripture verse of the pornographer probably is, "There is nothing hidden that shall not be revealed," and he goes to work with might and main to make public every aspect of private parts and does it by using the crudest type of language.

C. S. Lewis claimed that in all literature the so-called four-letter words have been the vocabulary of farce and vituperation. The reason is that four-letter words depict people in terms of their bodily functions so a man or woman is reduced to mere animal functioning, which is just fine for the pornographer.

In many ways the works of pornography are an attack upon traditional or establishment values, and semantics have frequently been a weapon in the hands of would be revolutionaries.

The Bolshevik Lenin emphasized the use of language as a means of tearing down the outmoded establishment. In his communication methods he used the most brutal language to attack his opponents who are referred to as swine, offal, treacherous dogs, hyenas.

Lenin called his technique "intimidation by the word," and he described the use of words as, "It is not designed to convince, but to break the wings, not to correct a mistake of an opponent, but to annihilate him, to wipe him off the face of the earth."

Significantly in the course of the counter culture movement among radical students the use of four-letter words became the order of the day. What started as the free speech movement moved into a stage in which participants stood on soap boxes shouting out obscenities. This practice led to the whole enterprise being designated as *The Dirty Speech Movement.*

Without trying to see anything of a Communist plot about pornography, it certainly has some aspects of a well orchestrated assault on traditional values, and one of the weapons of this warfare is gutter language.

Dr. David Mace suggests that the word "intercourse" is of far greater value for describing sexual relations than any of the four-letter words. "It would be more appropriate to use the four-letter word which describes what a man does to a woman and not what a man and a woman do together. That's why I don't want to see the four-letter word made respectable. What's wrong with it is not just that it is considered vulgar but that it describes a concept of the sexual act that is male oriented and impersonal."

Almost as a footnote we might note there are some people who are experts with four-letter words. These individuals get on the phone with a woman and make sexual suggestions laced with gutter language. It seems as if these are generally men with inadequate personalities who are trying to bolster their ego and get their personal sexual stimulation by shocking a woman. The pornographers fit neatly into this category plus the additional motivation of lucrative income.

Perhaps we should refer to the musical adaptation of George Bernard Shaw's famous play on the use of langauge and quote the statement of Professor Henry Higgins, "Remember that you are a human being with a soul and the divine gift of articulate speech; that your native language is the language of Shakespeare and Milton and the Bible; and don't sit there crooning like a bilious pigeon."

Porno Violence

In his quest for variety the pornographer has to explore every avenue of human sexuality to provide something new. One of the very fruitful possibilities is sadomasochism.

A fairly typical situation is one in which the seductive girl leads the man to take her out to a lover's lookout where they find a secluded spot and she begins to initiate him into some wayout sexual activities.

In the midst of all this they are surprised by a gang of four men. Her partner struggles with the assailants, but a quick knock over the head leaves him unconscious. A man seizes hold of the girl and drags her out onto the ground nearby and whenever she struggles to escape punches her into submission. Then follows the detailed description of the simultaneous sexual assault of the four men who perform every conceivable abnormal act of sexuality on their victim.

And how does this subject of their cruel punching, clawing, and perverted sexual assault react?

Within herself, according to the pornographer, she thinks, "Oh do it. Rip me to pieces . . . isn't this what every girl dreams of secretly to herself?"

The pornographer's skill further manifests itself in the manner he portrays this girl as overcoming her inhibitions as she, "vibrates with delight from head to foot and when at last the whole process was concluded she lay there . . . remembering every priceless moment of her classic rape."

A part of this emphasis in pornography lies in its pre-occupation with such far out activities as scatology and uro-lagnia and the stories of whipping, chaining people, forcibly using hot enemas. This material of "bondage and discipline," as it is known in the trade, is pornography that is desperately sick.

As with so much of the pornographer's work, the portrayal of women as seen in these situations is completely false. One woman authority in the field states the situation, "Perhaps there is no greater source of serious misunderstanding than the assumption that women enjoy pain. This has been used to jus-tify a great deal of callous if not cruel treatment of women . . . Far from desiring brutal men, the evidence suggests that women would prefer men to be more kind and considerate."[2]

Super-Sexed Males

The complete unreality of pornography is clearly seen in the portrayal of masculine sexuality. The men who are the all im-portant figures of pornography, are sex athletes who have tre-mendous physical sexual equipment, the size of which is only exceeded by their erotic desire and capacity to function sex-ually.

The fantasy of an ejaculating phallus apparently has some peculiar stimulating effect upon certain males. Pornographic art panders to this interest and features the male's ejaculate with a favored portrayal of girls having been engaged in fellatio with semen on their face. How a sensitive girl would react to this type of experience would be questionable, but for certain males it is obviously stimulating. Similarly, in the stories of erotic literature the ejaculate is of a quantity that is simply not biologically possible.

The description of the phallus is worthy of a loquacious guide at an Italian Art Museum and uses hyperbole and meta-phor that emphasize an appearance running the gamut from awesome and threatening to fascinating and enticing with every vein and contour minutely described. When it comes to size, all the superlatives of the English language are called into ser-vice ignoring the findings of Masters and Johnson that phallic sizes are fairly standard.

The male of pornography has unlimited powers of endur-

A THREE-FOLD TRUST

RESPONSIBILITY OF FEEDING THE MIND

RESPONSIBILITY OF FEEDING THE BODY

RESPONSIBILITY OF FEEDING THE SOUL

"LET THE CHILDREN COME TO ME, DO NOT HINDER THEM; FOR TO SUCH BELONGS THE KINGDOM OF GOD."— *CHRIST* (MARK 10:14)

ance, engaging in constant series of sexual encounters with all the stamina of a marathon runner. In actual fact the male has a limited capacity for primary sex, particularly when compared to the female.

To further rub salt into the wound, some authorities in the field have come up with what must be, to male pornography fans, a rather disconcerting conclusion that much of this pre-occupation with the phallus and marathon performances may really be a cover up for the male's anxiety about his masculinity and the lurking fear of impotency.

Seductive Females

The woman of pornography is a mythical female who exists nowhere but in the pornographer's imagination. All of the normal characteristics so frequently found amongst women, modesty, restraint, and sex anxiety have been suddenly jettisoned to portray a female who is passionate, seductive, and spends her waking hours fighting a consuming lust that can only be satisfied by successfully bedding a partner—any partner—animal or human.

One such portrayal is of the much acclaimed actress working on the movie set under fierce heat of the Kleig lights. No sooner has the producer's last "cut" been uttered than she hurries off to her dressing room, dons her most provocative revealing mini-skirt and see-through blouse, and heads out for a bar where she is reasonably sure no one will know her and realize that instead of a prim actress she is really a lustful nymphomaniac.

In the bar she spots a handsome man, broad-shouldered, well-built, and giving off vibrations indicating he has a bountiful sexual endowment. In less time than it takes to say "libido" she finds a seat alongside him at the bar and asks him to light her cigarette. As he leans over, she sidles up to him giving a "take me" signal, and they quickly decide to go to his apartment.

Once in the car she makes a move towards him, and he to her, and they become so deeply involved in heavy petting that, when they are stopped by a red light, they provide a spectacle for the gawking bus passengers.

Arriving at his apartment, he proceeds to tear off her dress—in these stories the subjects apparently have never learned the simple process of operating zips or buttons—she breaks loose from his eager hands, and he chases her around the room periodically tearing off portions of her clothing. He hurls himself after her and brings her down with a flying tackle, fortuitously across the bed, and they launch into a whole series of orgiastic experiences.

Then there is that voracious, lacivious female who sets about to seduce the unsophisticated young man. She is frequently a woman of some social status, actress wife of a tycoon, famous artist. The young man, well-built and giving indication of great virility but apparently not too bright intellectually, works as a humble messenger who comes to deliver the flowers of an admirer.

One glimpse of this personification of masculinity decides this female. She must have him. So begins a series of ploys by which she works on the rather dull youth. Filled with amazement he finally capitulates to the desires of his seductress who, the moment she has satisfied her lust, dismisses him with an ample monetary reward in hand.

Most seduction scenes involve an ambiguity. The seducer is overpowered by a tremendous urge and goes all out to carry out a carefully formulated plan by maneuvering a victim into a position from which escape is virtually impossible. He need not have worried. His victim is no victim at all. She is welcoming his advances and not only surrenders to him but is grateful for the service that he has performed. The only negative note in the whole experience is in the mind of the skeptical reader who may inwardly wonder why ever on earth the so-called victim remained virginal as long as she did.

These portrayals overlook the nature of feminine sexual response which is not nearly so genitally focused as is that of the male.

A woman writing on the subject has pointed out that the common temptation of a male writer is to assume that someone of the opposite sex is like onself and may naively project the pattern of one's own sexual reaction upon the female. She takes up a feminine view of sexual experiences, "Many women enjoy cuddling as much as or more than coitus. A woman approaching her husband for cuddling, however, is likely to get coitus instead. One young woman with a strong need for cuddling precipitated a sexual problem in her marriage because of her continual desire for body contact. Her husband interpreting her behavior as a desire for coitus, exhausted himself and ended by accusing his wife of excessive sex drive."[3]

Bestiality

Another of the widely held prohibitions in most societies is against bestiality—humans engaging in sexual activity with animals. It follows that bestiality will provide an opportunity for the pornographer.

One treatment of this theme tells of a woman who sees a blue movie that shows two girls and a dog engaged in sexual practices. The idea so captivates her mind that she is determined to seek such an experience.

She goes out and seduces another gal—or thinks she does—but her companion takes the seducer to an apartment where she introduces her dog and helps her new friend not only perform as a lesbian but also initiates her into sexual activity with her dog. As the story develops, the subject describes herself in her own words as becoming "sex mad" for activity with women, dogs, or girls.

A very natural and favored setting for the bestiality theme is down on the farm. Here the country boys or girls engage in sexual activity with the conveniently available goats, donkeys, horses, or cattle.

Believing one picture is worth more than a thousand words, many of the visual types of pornography have majored in sexual practices with dogs, pigs and even snakes. Interest in this type of material may be gauged by its price tag. Pornographers are notorious exploiters of as much as the trade will bear and quickly jack up prices in response to demand. Some books of visual portrayals of bestiality carry prices as high as $15.00 per copy.

Observation of the way in which the pornographer uses livestock as a means of stimulating sexuality may cause the reader to speculate about the use of the expression, "higher animal" to describe man. While it may reinforce the use of the word "animal" in this context it certainly leaves a question as to the validity of the adjective "higher."

Detailed Description

In pornographic writings the description of any individual is almost completely focused upon sexual functioning and this is generally portrayed in considerable detail.

Women are described in terms of their voluptuous figures that give off messages of sexuality and any girl who is going to amount to anything must have an enormous bustline that is supposed to indicate her sensuous nature.

In the accounts of feminine sexual response a major emphasis lies on responses that are similar to those of the male.

When feminine genitalia is described in detail, the focus is on erection of nipples or oversized clitoris and copious discharges. Some of their writings give descriptions of a female orgasm in which the female ejaculates in the same manner as the male.

The orgasm itself is a chaotic body wracking experience that goes into action like a series of explosions. It is so joyous, and at the same time devastating, that the female may cry for mercy from the male so that she can collapse into sleep and respite from the delightful torment of the experience.

Similarly with the descriptions of the male. We have already noted not only the emphasis on the improbable size of the phallus and testes and the impossible quantities of ejaculate but the complete distortion of sexuality involved in these concerns.

However it is the feminine form which is displayed as some beacon light radiating a sexuality and luring on the male with a prospect of sex orgy.

The outstanding example of this is seen in the show biz aspects of pornography where strippers take off their clothes, parade before an audience of males, and make suggestive body movements that radiate a message of sensuous desires.

One study of these girls showed they were mainly engaged in this work because of ample physical endowment and the easy money it offered. What was going through a girl's mind while she did her bumps and grinds? One responded, "I make up the grocery list."

In what must be the crowning blow to the masculine ego, a big proportion of these girls had virtually no interest in sex with males—whom they thought of as callous exploiters, and sixty per cent of them acknowledged that they were lesbians.

The Skill of Eroticising

The picturesque biblical statement, "Whithersoever the carcass is there will the vultures gather," is nowhere more vividly demonstrated than in the productions of the pornographers that follow hard on the heels of the publication of any volume reporting the results of investigations into human sexuality. These productions frequently show the skill of eroticising that is the hallmark of the pornographer.

When Masters and Johnson undertook their monumental study into the human sexual experience, they claim they made every effort to avoid the sensational, but no sooner did word of

PORNOGR... OBSCENITY "X" MOVIES

"WHEN LUST HATH CONCEIVED, IT BRINGETH FORTH SIN: AND SIN, WHEN IT IS FINISHED, BRINGETH FORTH DEATH." —JAS. 1:15

LUST

JACK HAMM

their enterprise begin to leak out than the vultures came flapping across the sky to circle for the kill.

One of the most objectionable and morally indefensible techniques of the Masters and Johnson therapy was the use of women as surrogates in the treatment of masculine sexual dysfunction. This part of the program has since been discontinued, but it provided the basis for a book allegedly written by a woman who claims she worked in these treatment programs and served as a surrogate wife.

Of course it is an "as told to" book, with names of both the "sexual therapist" and the author to whom she told her story conveniently in quotes to show they are pseudonyms.

The account uses all the skills of the pornographer. Despite her association with Masters and Johnson, "Valerie X" has never learned the adult language with which to describe human genitalia and the processes of sexual relations. She was so oblivious to all that was being said in the medical circles of the conferences she attended that she felt it was necessary to use gutter language in her description of her varied experiences.[4]

Let any factual report appear on some form of sexual activity and the material is quickly picked up by a writer who selects that which best suits his purposes then goes to town on the eroticising process which involves using the themes and techniques already discussed in this chapter. His peculiar skill lies in capitalizing on the erotic potential and turning facts into sexual aphrodisiacs.

Pornographic Art

The letters "A-R-T" apparently spell opportunity to the pornographer. When some of the early pornographic films were imported from abroad they were referred to as "Art" films and the places where the films were screened were labeled "art" theaters.

Perhaps because artists have always claimed a certain freedom and license in their work many a pornographer has hastened to jump on to the band wagon with his "art."

This has led to the market being flooded with books that sometimes have a few stories, others that are nothing but pictures, yet others are large and known as the "Annuals" with the inference that they are the accumulation of a whole year of collecting and editorializing.

Pornographic art has many of the characteristics of the literature used for the same purpose. They are sexual aphrodisiacs and must have presentations that are sexually titillating.

Apparently the feminine breast has the greatest sexual appeal to the male, and so the women in the "art" work are generally bountifully endowed in this area. To make the breast more obvious they may be partly suntanned, or the model may wear a see-through bra. She is frequently bent forward to make the most of things or has her busts carefully taped underneath so they will show to best advantage. One particular publication specializes in pictures of girls holding a nipple.

There was a time when the pictures in pornography magazines gave the impression that girls had no pubic hair. Then one magazine added it, and it wasn't long before others followed, and pubic hair marked the great leap forward in the pornographer's art.

The natural progression was what some call "split beaver" and other "wide open pictures." In these everything is revealed, and girls pose in almost unbelievable positions so that their legs are spread wide giving a worm's eye view of genitals. In others that seem like advertisements for a school for contortionists, the models take up poses in which the anus and genitals are paraded for the voyeur.

To further enhance the art work there are certain props to heighten the Peeping Tom's reactions. A remarkable number of the models wear black garter belts and hose, some feature net stockings and see-through blouses, others abbreviated red plastic suits, still others are adorned in black knee length boots and black gloves as their only clothing.

The subjects for portrayal in pornographic art are acting out the same themes as the writers have depicted. Girls in all types of poses majoring on exposure of primary and secondary sex organs, simulated sexual intercourse, man and woman, girl and girl, boy and boy, black and white, and sundry mixtures, groups copulating, males and females masturbating, sadomasochistic practices.

Like the writers, the pornographic artist is committed to techniques of sexual arousal.

Convenient Oversights

While the ability of the pornographer is seen in his modus operandi as he presents themes and ideas, his expertise is also demonstrated by the way in which he avoids mentioning some aspects of human experience.

One of the brazen claims of pornography is—"we tell it all—just the way it really is."

This is the big lie.

The problem with pornography is not that they tell too much—they tell too little.

The stories of the pornographer are incomplete presentations that show dramatic sexual experiences without bothering to tell the reader about the final outcome of the event.

A fairly typical story tells about the country girl who comes to the big city and after a few amorous adventures becomes part of the staff of a house of prostitution. In this role she deceives both patrons and the madam, on the side she seduces sundry boys, helps cheat customers of the establishment. After a colorful career an aged John leaves her a large sum of money, a handsome young man falls in love with her, they marry, have a family and live happily ever after.

No pregnancy—no venereal disease—no pimps—no police raids—no sadistic patrons—every aspect of reality is ignored.

Chapter Four

Skin Flicks, Roughies, Kinkies and Ghoulies— The Movie Mess

Whenever I turn my mind back to my boyhood days I invariably think of the great event of the week—going to the movies.

How well I recollect the early days in my native Australia of hectic Saturday afternoons, peanuts, and Eskimo Pies, sitting on the hard seats, no arm rests, just backs, providing the exact opportunity for mischievous kids to give a mighty push at one end of the seat, sending those at the other end into a wild scrambled heap. Cheering on the heroic cowboy, and his horse Silver King, we were so carried away as to yell warnings to the hero, "Look out, Fred, they've strung a rope across the trail," and as the lights later came up following the inevitable serial, drained of all emotion, reluctantly trudging out of the crude building to face an apprehensive week, speculating about the fate of the lumberman, unheeding, unconscious, and drifting towards the thundering rapids . . . "Don't miss next week's episode."

The later days when the cinema was king and the place to which to take your girlfriend, the plain barn-like building replaced by ornate temples, dimly lit to provide a place of worship for the devotees of the silver screen, elaborately uniformed attendants maneuvering through their carefully rehearsed paces while the grand organ rose miraculously out of the floor, its spotlighted player dramatically hovering over the keyboard to coax out popular songs that led to a crushing crescendo.

War years in the Pacific Islands sitting in the open air on gasoline cans, shrouded in a poncho to ward off the incessant rains, the air redolent with the heady aroma of mosquito repellent, moved by the glimpses of civilian life in its most idealized form, all the time dependent on balky projectors, fragile film that broke so easily, coughing generators and operators as heroic as front line fighters. Their noble creed—no matter what wind or rain or storm or number of film separations, while even one soldier elected to remain to watch, the show continued on.

Apparently I'm not the only one who looks back to another era with a certain nostalgia. Nor is it just the amateur moviegoer who feels this way. No less a movie celebrity than Katherine Hepburn after seeing two of the new generation of films laments, "It's pornography. Nothing more or less than pornography. It appeals to the lowest possible level of human experience. I think it's atrocious." Zeroing in on one of these films she adds, "It's a picture about lust. That's all it is—lust. Two dull self-centered men and their sex problem."

During the early halcyon years of the movie industry some 80 million people attended the movies at least once a week. The industry itself was almost completely dominated by five studios. They enforced a regulatory code through an organization known as the Production Code Administration—P.C.A. Until 1948 approximately 95 per cent of films released in the U.S.A. were passed and approved by this organization.

The whole system was struck a decisive blow by the landmark court decision that compelled the production companies to divest themselves of their exhibiting outlets. Thus it became possible for a producer to find movie houses willing to exhibit films that had not received the P.C.A. code of approval that had previously been a prerequisite for screening in a "majors" outlet.

To this time it had generally been assumed that a movie that did not have the seal of approval would be doomed to failure. Then in 1953, what has been described as an "innocuous comedy" entitled *The Moon Is Blue* dealt rather frivolously with the theme of adultery—no depiction however—and the seal of approval was withheld. Instead of failure the movie turned out to be a booming success and so gave a new perspective to the rating system.

Something Childish About Playing In Mud Holes

A whole series of factors entered in to complicate the situation. Foreign films, generally referred to as Art Films, had come on to the market without the code of approval, and courts began striking down the powers of local censors. The greatest incursion of all, however, came with the arrival of the ubiquitous television set which now appeared in American homes.

Speaking of Ratings

X-RATED
"DOWN, DOWN, DOWN TO THE GUTTER"

"LEWDNESS IS SPORT FOR THE STUPID; BUT TO A MAN OF SENSE IT IS DISGUSTING." — PROV. 10:23 (N.E.B. & MOF. TRS.)

JACK HAMM

In about the same ratio, as television sets became a part of the family furnishings, movie theater attendance began to decline. The movie industry looked anxiously around for some way to pull the television viewers away from their sets and back to the theater and they hit upon the magic formula—greater quantities of and more explicit sexual depictions.

The movie producers apparently abandoned the "family" market and began exploring themes that had previously been

"AS HE THINKETH IN HIS HEART, SO IS HE." —PROV. 23:7

"off limits." So came drug addiction, political dissent, racism, and anti-establishment movies. But sex provided the greatest potential as the producers began to explore the possibilities of a great variety of sexual themes and portrayals.

In the midst of all this new freedom it might have been imagined that a rating system was the last thing that the movie industry would have wanted, but a cloud was appearing on the horizon—the spectre of outside censorship.

As a reaction to the threat of some outside evaluation of their products, the MPAA (Motion Picture Association of America) decided on some objectives to guide in setting up a new code and rating system. They were "(1) To encourage artistic expression by expanding creative freedom, (2) To assure that freedom which encourages the artist to remain responsible and sensitive to the standards of a larger society."[1]

The new regulating body for the industry now replaced the old P.C.A. and was known as the Code and Rating Administration of C.R.A., and from their experimentation emerged a new rating system to guide the consumer in his selection of a movie. This system is set out in Chart A.

THE C.R.A. RATING SYSTEM AS OF JANUARY 1970

Rating	Restrictions	Content
"G"	All ages admitted.	Sexually pure, little beyond conventional embracing and kissing.
*"GP"	All ages admitted. Parental guidance suggested.	Moderately explicit indication of sex. Originally no nudity, later "brief flashes" or "long shots." No discussions or dramatizations of perversions. Premarital sex or adultery punished by moral compensation. Minimum amount of vulgarity.
"R"	Restricted under 17 Requires accompanying parent.	Breast and buttock nudity. Full nudity not allowed (1970) Touching and caressing breasts. Simulated intercourse. Any discussion of sex within bounds of good taste.
"X"	None under 17 admitted. (Age limit may vary in certain areas.)	Anything that can't be "G" "GP" or "R"

*Later changed to PG.

Even with such a flexible rating system there has been a tendency for the industry to move away from the "G" films. The overall trend of the industry has been towards releasing sex-oriented pictures. Of all the major producers only one, Buena Vista, which distributes the productions of Walt Disney studios, has not released any so-called "adult" movies but has kept its entire production to those rated "G."

A whole series of low budget films have been produced, which in the trade, in a moment of refreshing uncharacteristic frankness, are known as "exploitation" films. Other terms include "sexploitation," "adults only," or "skin flicks."

"Roughies" were the films emphasizing the sadistic note with women as the victims, then moved towards portraying women as the irrepressible aggressors and included nymphomaniacs, perverse lesbians, professional prostitutes, all in pursuit of masculine victims. They generally ended unhappily for the women, but not before they had been involved in a wide variety of erotic behavior and subjected to close examination by the camera.

A whole series produced later on were known as "kinkies" and explored the field of sexual aberration. They majored on the "shocking details" of such themes as fetishism and sado-masochism with those terrible women out after the unsuspecting male.

Another popular type has been the *ghoulies* that made their major play on violence.

The producers of the exploitation movies have shown considerable flexibility as they exhibit their films in any way that is going to increase box office receipts. Most of these films are released in two versions commonly known as "hot" and "cool." The "cool" version is toned down and provided for those exhibitors who prefer less explicit sex. As one exploitation director-producer puts it, "If the customer is important enough we are delighted to make it cooler certainly. But that is self-censorship—In order to get a new account who is important enough, worth making up an additional print or cutting an existing print, of course, we're going to do it."[2]

The same subtlety enters into the promotion of the "exploitation" movies. They have encountered difficulties with newspapers that won't carry their ads so they make extensive use of trailers—previews. The technique is to run in a trailer showing the coming attractions. These are frequently quite long—6-9 minutes. In some instances four to six trailers are used, and these are frequently so skillfully done that some customers reported they enjoyed the trailers more than the main feature.

The exploitation segment of the industry which calls itself the Adult Film Association of America (AFAA) has set up a code of conduct which reads: "Recognizing that motion pictures are a vital and established medium of communication in the United States of America and that persons privileged to engage in this form of expression have certain well defined responsibilities to the general public, we acknowledged these responsibilities and do hereby pledge:

1. That films of Adult Subject Matter will be exhibited to Adult Audiences and that persons not of adult age will not be admitted.

2. That the definition of an "Adult" is that designation set by the constituted authorities of this community, but in no event any person under the age of 18 years.

3. That we will exhibit only films that are in conformity with the Free Speech Provisions of the Constitution of the United States of America.

4. That we will respect the privacy of the General Public in our Advertising and Public Displays."[3]

A more innocuous statement of a code than this would be difficult to imagine. As they see it, the First Amendment places no restrictions on what may be screened. About the only thing the Code is intimating is that the films will not be exhibited to anyone under the age of eighteen.

It was inevitable that the success of the exploitation movies would affect the "general release" people, and so came the "hybrid" film which, although originally an exploitative production, moved into the "general release" category. Then appeared the "new genre" films which majored on the great hypocrisy of the pornographic world by masquerading as éducational, advertising sex education for adults. One such was *Man and Wife* demonstrating copulatory techniques for "married couples." The response lead the industry to come up with a series of similar productions: *The Marriage Manual, The Art of Marriage.*

This opened the door for documentary type productions that purported to give the patrons some good information as to what was going on in the big wide world. Examples: *Wide*

Open Copenhagen 1970, Pornography in Denmark, Sexual Freedom in Denmark. While ostensibly set in Denmark, it was not the Danish topography that was being viewed but rather the most explicit types of sexuality screened up to this time. These films contained such shots as erect male genitals, close-up of coitus, fondling of genitals, and anal genital contact. Almost all the taboos that hitherto had been observed in the public market were ignored.

The Key Element of the Rating System

The pious claim of the movie industry has been that parents bear the main responsibility for deciding what movies their children are going to view. Consequently, as Randall puts it, "Informing the public, particularly parents, of the relative suitability of a film for children and youth is perhaps the key element in the entire rating system."[4]

But, when a survey of theater advertisements was made, it was revealed that the statement of the rating was either absent (34.4%) or unsatisfactory in 44.8% of movie advertisements. As the investigator commented, "The insufficiency percentage of 44.8% is even more noteworthy because of the near absolute control the film producer has over advertising and because of the ease with which ratings—ones that are both correct and graphically non-defective—can be included in the ads."[5]

There is one rating that can get a good display, and that is "X." One researcher notes the hyperinforming that sometimes takes place to lure in the committed voyeur. Despite the restrictions on size of rating symbols in some of the adult theaters the "X" is up to five times the size of the title of the film. Some ads appear with a large "X" superimposed over the photograph of a woman. In the ad copy some of them go all out, "XXX—so adult one X is not enough," "Two hot ones—X," "The film that goes beyond X."

Altogether, the advertising of ratings of films has become an instrument in the hands of the movie industry to be used when it suits and in the manner that will improve the box office take.

At the Theater Door

An important part of a rating system is to be found in the way it is administered. If the system states, "Anyone under 17 must be accompanied by a parent," or "No one under 17 ad-

mitted," the evidence of the sincerity of the statement will be seen in the way the exhibitor enforces the restrictions.

A recent article in the *New York Times* reported the policies of some newspapers who, because of their dissatisfaction with the movie rating system, were refusing to take all advertisements for X-rated movies. The writer took issue with this policy and reviewed the reason for rating films as ". . . to assist parents in policing their children's viewing and—in the case of

X-rated films—to prohibit theater managers from admitting minors to certain films."[6]

Note the word "prohibiting." A survey showed that the admission standard that anyone attending the theater should be wearing shoes was far more rigidly enforced than any of the requirements as to age and being accompanied by a parent. Reason—to prevent lawsuits resulting from cut feet.

In one survey only 21.2 percent of the theaters visited had an effective rigorous check on who would be admitted. Closer scrutiny revealed that many of the employees in the box office, and those taking the tickets at the entrance, had no clear idea as to what the rating system really was.

Moreover many of the employees, ushers, doormen, ticket sellers, and concessionaires were in their late teens and would have been required to turn away young people just a few years younger than themselves. Along with this went a lack of interest in the work they were doing. Some of them described enforcement of the rating system as, "a lot of trouble," and "a lot of baloney."

One investigator reported, "On the basis of the 40 theaters observed in the three state area, it cannot be said that the rating system was being well enforced at the box office."[7]

In many ways the whole rating system represents a reluctant gesture by the movie industry. After all the pious talk about concern for children, guidance for parents, means of providing a milieu for artistic expression, and giving the producers artistic sovereignty, the over-riding consideration was *economic.* As Randall says it, "Statements occasionally emitting from the industry that the rating system was formed primarily to advise parents and protect children can be discounted as attempts to make public relations capital."[8]

Family Night at the Movies

Just in case you haven't attended the local theater lately, you might be interested in a survey carried out by a prominent behavioral scientist who made a study of the movies screened during a four week period in a western city of 25,000 population. The city was politically moderately conservative and did not have any "porno" movie houses within its environs. Four raters with wide experience attended and viewed 37 films. Of

these 16% were rated "X", 24% rated "R", 46% rated "PG",
and 14% bore the classification of "G".

In these films the raters tabulated 566 sexual acts which
came out at about 15 per film. The type of activity portrayed
can be seen in Table B.[9]

TABLE B
Summary of Sexual Acts/Displays in 37 Motion Pictures Viewed in a One Week Period

Rank Order	Type of Sexual Display	Number
1	Nudity (front and/or back, partial and/or whole)	168
2	Kissing, embracing, body contact	90
3	Bed scene with sexual connotations	49
4	In undergarments in sexual context	36
5	Seductive exhibition of body	32
6	Verbalizing sex interest/intentions	36
7	Caressing another's organs (including breasts):	
	Clothed	27
	Nude	21
8	Undressing	34
9	Intercourse, explicit	19
10	Intercourse, suggested/implied	17
11	Homosexual activity	11
12	Intercourse, oral-genital	7
13	Toilet scene	5
14	Rape	4
15	Obscene gesture	4
16	Masturbation	3
17	Sexual sadism/masochism	3
		566

Although at first glance we might be heartened to notice that
only three of the films dealt with sadomasochistic practices, we
might also note that sex scenes are actually outnumbered by
depictions of violence of which there were 833 incidents in the
37 films.

Dr. Cline, who supervised this piece of research, reached
some interesting conclusions about the ideas of love, sex, and
marriage presented by these particular movies.

"In sixty percent of the films premarital and extra-marital
sexual relations were presented as 'normal, acceptable, and
desirable.' Seventy percent of the heroes or male leads were
presented as being to some degree sexually promiscuous be-

Dump Ground

fore and/or outside of marriage). Seventy-two percent of those films having a heroine also presented her as being somewhat sexually promiscuous (before and/or outside of marriage). Only one film (3%) of those analyzed, suggested or depicted sexual relations between a man and a woman legally married to each other. In sixty-five percent of the films the hero and heroine who are not married to each other have sexual relations. In some cases they are married to others, in other cases not. In other words, the model of sex presented in American cinema is almost entirely 'illicit' with an almost total rejection of the notion that sex might occur between men and women married to each other.

"In only twenty-two percent of the films were any of the principal figures seen engaged in what might be termed healthy and reasonably satisfying marriages. Another twenty-seven percent of the films presented the main characters in pathological marital situations and the remaining fifty-one percent of the films showed all of the key characters as unmarried or not essentially involved in marriage. In other words, models of healthy marriage and marital interaction are present in only a fairly small minority of films."[10]

Problem Areas of Movies

One of the frankest acknowledgments of the hyprocrisy of the movie industry comes of all places from *Playboy* magazine, "Many courts around the country, however, continue to apply the customary three point yardstick—community standards, redeeming social values, and absence of prurient interest—to measure films' morality, with the result that today's producers and distributors of frank exploitation films are selling their wares by solemnly, if often hypocritically, stating that sex is the farthest thing from their mind, that their pictures are therapeutic, informational, moral, uplifting, even on occasion, patriotic. The sex just happens to be there."[11]

Apparently even acting in these movies with simulated sex brings its own difficulties. Equity, the British Actors Union, has appointed inspectors to watch over the filming of some of the mass sex scenes to make sure the participants follow the directions given in the script. The action was taken after five actresses complained that they were sexually assaulted during a shooting scene from a movie rather appropriately titled *The Devils*.[12]

A strange aspect of the movie scene is the claim that family type movies "G" die at the box office. Randall, in his study of the gross takings of movies for the years 1968-9, showed that although "G" movies represented only 29% of the films released, they accounted for 38.4% of the gross takings. As a

LANDSLIDE ?

category the "G" films brought in more income than any other single category. Of course they probably cost more to produce. Randall comments, " . . . as a group "G" films tend to have consistently higher grosses than either "PG" or "R" films. . . . The data indicate that "G" films do not die at the box office as often claimed, in some quarters in the industry."[13] Is the diet of non-family films because of consumer demand, or are we being propagandized by people who are trying to foist

**You may not prevent its flying overhead,
but you can prevent its nesting in your hair.**

their tastes on the general public or trying to create a whole new market?

Today's movie becomes tomorrow's TV program, and herein lies a problem of the first order. Many of these films were made for a special audience and it was *not the family*. Aware that families were sitting at home in front of their television sets, the producers went farther out in producing non-family and in many instances anti-family movies. But television has a voracious appetite for material and it has increasingly moved to the movie industry for films that can be used to fill up the evening hours, and the very films produced in the first instance for anything but the family are those that are available.

In George Orwell's *1984* every home had an all-seeing eye by which Big Brother peered in to see what was happening. Television is the reverse of this situation and lets the movie industry's Big Brother present his visualized messages which unfortunately are all too frequently jammed full of violence and way-out sex.

In discussion with a thoughtful man about pornography on films and TV he said, "Yes, I can see what you mean but why this preoccupation with sex? How about violence. Shouldn't we be concerned about that?"

The answer is resounding, "Yes, we should and must."

Whenever the portrayals of sexuality become more deviant it follows like the night to day that aggression, violence, sadism, and masochism move in as subjects for presentation.

Cline gives an excellent evaluation of violence in films.

"In faulting the violence to be found in the American cinema, the most telling argument against it is not its sheer volume, but that too little is taught or modeled of the real nature of violence and how to control it. Rarely is there shown the impact, the aftermath, or follow-up, of all those people so neatly dispatched, or injured . . . as it might be in real life. We don't see the grieving family of the father who was so efficiently killed by the hero, or the man with the damaged spine, now unemployed and crippled for life by the slug in the lower vertebra, or the adolescent girl who was gang raped, which so titillated and turned on the male audience, but who in real life is likely to have many years of acute marital problems arising out of her resulting sexual frigidity.

Thus the American movie ethic equates courage and masculinity with violence, and the solution of problems with impulsive aggressive action.

The cinema teaches us the norms, values, and customs of its mythical society. It presents us with partially true and partially distorted images of our environment.[14]

In an American home, as far as television is concerned, at least, the child is often king—did you ever try to watch the news when cartoons are on another station?—and channels are selected in many homes at the child's behest. Moreover, TV has often become the economical baby sitter, and it is open season on children for whatever fare the networks put on the airwaves.

Yet there is a grave dissatisfaction with the situation. In November, 1972, Californians were asked to vote on a proposition that would have placed strict rules on pornography and obscenity. The law was misrepresented, the movie industry poured money into a $530,000 campaign against the proposition, and conservatives like John Wayne were enlisted against it. ("You don't cut off a foot to save a toe.") Despite this, one out of every three voters cast a ballot for a new law.

The prospects of such laws helps to keep the movie industry's feet to the fire. The newspapers reported about the Californian experience. "The proposed law threw a scare into the film industry." Good. It might be a good idea to adapt the title of one of the popular movies, "Let's Scare the Movie Industry to Death."

There are mumblings within the industry itself. George Cukor who gave us *My Fair Lady* says, "My quarrel with some of the current films is that they present sex so unattractively . . . . Today's films present a distorted view. They have gone too far and have alienated a great segment of the movie audience."

The citizen concerned about his children and those of other people, a healthy concept of sexuality, a real image of motherhood, and the stability of his society cannot help but be concerned about the movie industry. He needs to be aware of "The Need to Complain Louder," and keep the pressure on so that he can feel comfortable when he takes his wife and family to the movies.

Chapter Five

Licensed Licentiousness—the Swingers

Like an exotic tropical plant, pornography has produced some improbable fruits, none of which is more peculiar than the phenomenon generally referred to as "swinging." Just in case the word "swinger" takes you back to memories of dangling over the old swimming hole, happy cries of children at the park, or a nostalgic recollection of the front porch on a warm summer evening, we had better note that the modern definition of swinging is, "having sexual relations as a couple with at least one other individual."

The term "group sex" can include a lot of activities. Many of the communes that have sprung up across the country accept nudism as a way of life, and group sex is the order of the day, but this activity has a strong ideological basis. The practice stems from the idea that the members are living in a community where everything is shared and no one has his own private possessions. It naturally follows that two people committed just to each other will be seen as going against the ideological tide. Sometimes, in an effort to communalize the children, a girl will have intercourse with a number of men during her fertile days, thus making sure that no one will know who is the biological father.

Several investigators have concluded that group marriages are not very durable, and the failure rate is one out of two. The reason: "Group marriage is a marathon that does not end, it takes real commitment to genuine substantial, and unrelenting personal growth to really make it function and work."[1]

The swingers have tried to avoid the commune and group marriage pitfalls as they have developed their distinctive attitude toward sex.

67

Swinging takes place on a number of levels, and pornography plays its distinctive role as the activity is publicized and promoted through books, magazines, and movies.

The non-specialized media lays the groundwork for swinging. In what is normally thought of as a respectable newspaper or magazine an article appears on the subject of wife swapping or group sex. On the basis of being an investigative report of the goings on in a wider society, group activities are discreetly discussed as an account of "how the other half lives."

Reading one of these articles one spouse, generally the male, says, "Oh, boy, that sounds interesting, where do I find out more?"

And the marketers of pornography are standing by to offer a helping hand with several different types of publications.

The so-called "girlie" magazines fulfill an important role in the movement. These carry a number of articles on group sex experiences and wife swapping, and at this level it is presented as a very glamorous, desirable, and exciting experience.

At yet another level comes the swingers' magazine with a variety of articles on sex, much advertising of sexually stimulating material, and most important of all for the prospective swinger, a whole series of individual swingers' advertisements. Most of these types of publications are not well printed, sometimes on poor quality paper, but it is the lengthy list of couples' or even singles' advertisements that is the significant point.

If the publication is of a tabloid type, it may sell for as little as twenty-five cents, making its money out of advertising. An advertisement may have as many as twenty-five words and cost $5.00—with the special privilege that single men, and especially single women, may advertise without charge. The respondent who answers an advertisement is required to write to the paper and enclose a dollar plus ten cents for postage.

Yet another level (let the reader judge whether higher or lower) is reached in the specialized publications that cater to the swingers. This type of magazine is not available on general bookstands but is generally to be found in what are referred to as the "porno shops." They are carefully encased in sealed cellophane packages, for, although the publishers of these magazines are broadminded and want to encourage people to admire the human form so freely displayed in their magazine, they don't want any freeloaders. If people won't pay the exorbitant prices, they are not going to look.

Some of the magazines may cost up to $4.50, and they often are in the business of running their own swinging clubs to which members belong by paying dues which may be as high as $10.00 per year.

One survey among swingers showed that a swingers' publication played a large part in initiating almost all of them into swinging practices. The first step generally lay in acquiring a swingers' paper or magazine. From that time onward this so-called literature served to support and reinforce the swingers in their new "way of life."

Without this type of pornography swinging as a movement would die. One investigator has concluded that 95 per cent of potential swingers in the country and 100 per cent of those in the rural areas make their contacts through swingers' magazines.

The advertisements in these publications are frequently classified and listed under the headings of the various states where the advertisers live. A survey of these ads shows that they might well be the product of a Lonely Hearts Club public relations man with the essential difference that like Noah's animals many of them go two by two.

A sample ad reads:

Busty
Attractive couple, participating husband,
Caucasians, seek meeting with couples and
single females for threesomes. Please send
photos and phone.

When Dr. Land invented the Polaroid camera, he probably never dreamed that it would become the favored instrument with swingers. Almost with monotonous regularity the ads refer to "Polaroids," "enclose Polaroids," "can send Polaroids." One observer notes it may be more than coincidence that a recent model in the Polaroid line is called the "Swinger." Many of the advertisements in swingers' magazines have accompanying pictures. Of these pictures one investigator remarks, "Often the ads are accompanied by a picture which generally has only a remote resemblance to the real person,"[2] and another researcher reports that some couples send in photographs which are up to ten or twenty years old.[3]

Well, just look those pictures over.

If these are flattering pictures of the swingers, few of them are candidates for beauty contests, and most have no aesthetic reasons for removing their clothes.

One study of swingers showed that a big proportion of them had encountered unsatisfactory experiences somewhere along the line. The women had more problems than the men, particularly about getting started. Most of the women went along with a dominant husband, fearing that non-participation might mean losing him.

Many of the swingers' magazines tacitly acknowledge this problem with women and go all out to recruit females. One heading of a section reads:

> ATTENTION ALL LADIES!!
> Your ad free, accompanied by a photo.
> Don't delay send today.

Scattered throughout the publication are constant reminders to ladies of the free memberships available if they'll just write. In this particular publication women are always *ladies,* with the implication that the pathway to real gentility is to learn the art of swinging.

Sometimes a wife will advertise herself as being available. She indicates an understanding husband with such phrases as "husband approves," or, "husband likes to watch and join in." Perhaps the most pathetic note of all is that in an ad inserted by a husband, "wife is hesitant but willing to try."

This latter statement concerning an apprehensive wife is indicative of the way the whole "swinging scene" is a demonstration of a new *licensed licentiousness.*

Whatever way it may be expressed, the swinging scene is really an enormous hypocrisy by which people declare that their marriage license is like a hunting license, with an unlimited bag. Once in the fraternity, they conceive themselves as having access to a large group of partners with whom they can engage in a wide variety of sexual experimentation. In many swinging circles the participants insist that all the members of the group should be married and bring their spouses. However, the women are the losers again as some couples broaden the base by involving single girls as a third participant in their swinging sessions.

Of the pictures appearing in swingers' publications, about 80 per cent are of women, just a few men, some of whom are dressed in business suits, others with just head and shoulders view, some clad in bathing suits, and an occasional nude.

But wait, it won't be long. While visiting Holland recently I saw the more open-minded Dutch magazines displaying photographs that featured men and women contorting their bodies to show their genitals in much the same manner as anonymous models are doing in American hard core publications.

An examination of the ads in a swingers' magazine gives us some glimpses into the type of activity that characterizes swinging sessions.

> Attractive couple, early thirties, interested
> in meeting other couples, French culture,
> Greek, she is AC-DC, willing to try
> B & D.

Behind this terminology lies a whole gamut of sexual experiences. In one of the magazines the editor has even supplied a glossary to help newcomers to the swinging field.

Editor's Note: Many subscribers have written to inquire about the meaning of the abbreviations that are found in this magazine. Here is a brief glossary . . .

B & D	Bondage and Discipline (Tying up, whipping, and spanking)
S & M	Sado-Masochism (Pain either inflicted or endured)
French	Fellatio or Cunnilingus
Greek	Anal action
T V	Transvestite (Cross dressing)
Bi	Bi-sexual (Same as ac/dc)
Water sports	Urination activity or Golden Shower
SSAE	Stamped, self-address envelope

HAPPY HUNTING!

The frequent reference in ads to AC-DC girls raises the question about the part played by lesbian practices in swinging.

All indications are that a great number of masculine swingers get a kick out of watching women participating in lesbian activities, and this in turn gives rise to an unexpected by-product.

One researcher concluded that 92 per cent of the women attending swinging sessions had sexual experiences with another woman. Two thirds of them found the encounters very enjoyable and grew to prefer women over men as sexual partners.

This same investigator discovered that a group of women kept up their lesbian relationships outside the swinging experiences. And though the men may have enjoyed it at the party, they later saw it in a new light. One husband felt he had been excluded from his wife's emotional life. Another who, because of the titillating effect it had upon him, encouraged lesbian relationships at the beginning, was later gravely concerned about his wife's activities with her girl friend, which caused her to neglect their child. He also expressed resentment that he had to babysit while his wife went out with her girl friend on the homosexual escapades.

Swingers like to see themselves as broadminded and liberal with wide interests. They sometimes refer to themselves in exaggerated terms like "the beautiful people," "the jet set." The advertisements which they insert into swingers' magazines reflect this self-image. They advertise for partners who have "wide interests," "enjoy visiting galleries," "interested in the fine arts," "eating in good restaurants," and "attending concerts." The image is of glamorous openminded people who want to set up lasting social relationships of which sex is only a part and a minor part at that.

Between the swingers' self-image and the actual fact there is a great gulf. By and large, swingers are what one writer calls "a dull bunch" with almost no outside interests apart from sports, television, and an occasional magazine. One San Francisco housewife says, "Swinging saved my marriage because it gave me something to talk to my husband about."

Swingers pride themselves on being good, upright citizens, and when a group of female swingers get together at a social function, they talk about cooking, housecleaning, redecorating projects. But one observer noted when the discussion turned to children it was seldom that they boasted about their offsprings' achievements but rather a long whining complaint about the troubles the children brought, the expense of clothing, trouble with feeding, and the problems of school life.

The swingers are certainly not the gregarious socializers or scintillating conversationalists they imagine themselves to be.

In one area particularly swingers absolutely refuse to talk, for they have a fundamental taboo—no religious discussion.

Yet when quizzed, eighty-five per cent of them said they sent their children to Sunday School. Despite their frank intention of being sexually liberated they had an inner perception that their behavior would not square with even liberal religious views.

But one subject is discussed and rehashed a thousand times over—sex.

Participants are evaluated and categorized. The really attractive are known as "beautiful" or "great" while the unattractive and the indifferent performers are derisively labelled "moldy."

The whole enterprise is performance oriented.

We are used to contests, super bowls, jumping frogs, pancake eating, spitting, but swinging is the contest to end all contests, it is the Great Sex Olympiad. Each swinger in the group sessions is subjected to a process of evaluation of his or her technical performance. If he were brought to the function by another swinger, he feels he must come up with a performance that will justify his sponsor's confidence.

The situation is aggravated because performance takes place in the public arena of a gathering with others. Results of performances are discussed at length, and reports are spread around the group. The swinger has many questions in mind, "Did I do well? Was my partner satisfied? What sort of a report will they spread around?"

A type of seniority system develops with a corps of elite swingers. Beginners are referred to as "baby swingers," and some of the more experienced announced, "I don't swing with babies."

All of this leads to the struggle for a gold medal in the sexual olympics. Training means trying to keep one's figure in shape, consuming alleged aphrodisiacs, applying ointments. Ironically, particularly in the men, the constant struggle to perform may be self-defeating, often leaving the zealous male participant unable to function sexually and completely frustrated.

Possibly the most objectionable aspect of swinging is that it is sex without relationship. One rule, most generally followed, is that participants do not swing with any couple more than once. This means a constant pursuit of new prospects by introduction, advertising, and magazines, or joining an organization set up for the purpose. One observer noticed that most swingers live in mortal fear of some type of involvement with one of their partners.

This type of sex minimizes personal interaction. An observer of the swinging scene evaluates the attitude of the American swinger as being, "I don't mind if my partner has sexual intercourse with another individual as long as they do not have an emotional relationship."[4]

One of the most incredible aspects of all this is that the so-called act of "making love" has been completely divorced from any concept of love.

The one total prohibition is on using the term, "I love you." The swinger can say to his partner, "You have a terrific body," or, "I like the way you're built," or, "You really turn me on," but no terms of endearment, not so much as, "I care for you."

The fraudulently pious implication is that the swinger is so loyal to his spouse that he will not in any way become involved with another woman. Just his body for its sensory reaction, men and women return to the level of roosters and hens copulating at random in the barnyard.

One researcher reports on four girls who, after some swinging experiences, turned to prostitution. For them swinging brought complete disillusionment. Before swinging the idea of prostitution had not even entered their heads. Now after swinging they reasoned, "What is the difference? You have sex with a series of men to whom you had made no commitment. Why work as an amateur when I could get paid for it?" Very easily they moved over into the prostitution field.

Sexual activities are frequently of the way-out variety including fellatio, cunnilingus, anal intercourse, one woman with several men, several men with one woman, groups in "daisy chains" or "swallow the leader" formations. And in a modern industrialized and thoroughly mechanized America it would be expected that mechanization would enter the sex scene as it has with the introduction of the vibrator.

One researcher discovered that 62 per cent of swingers whom he interviewed had at some time or another used vibrators—purchased for other than the original stated purpose—or had been to parties where vibrators had been used for sexual experiences.

The husband of this thoroughly mechanized woman subsequently divorced her with the somewhat ludicrous comment, "I got tired of playing second fiddle to a vibrator."

We have entered upon an era of "swinging," and all of this has been encouraged by the media with a number of movies portraying swinging scenes and giving the impression that "everybody's doing it." But before you jump on the bandwagon it might be a good idea to consider some of the possible hazards of the swinging scene.

Swinging is primarily a process of pursuing a psycho-sexual will-o'-the-wisp. It generally begins with a male phantasy of the joys of uninhibited sexual experiences with a variety of voluptuous females. His wife frequently goes along with it to please him. All too frequently the will-of-the-wisp is too elusive and unattainable leaving complete frustration.

Because swinging is fundamentally a product of the masculine mind, many women find themselves strong-armed into this experience by their husbands. Masculine swingers are the sexual horse traders. They barter their wives. One researcher reported that when he discussed swinging with an experienced participant the man looked at his wife's figure and then said, "You won't have any trouble getting any woman you want."

As is so often the situation in the world of sex, the woman is all too frequently the loser.

Although most women enter the swinging scene in the hope of strengthening their marriage, in actual practice their activity may frequently engender a whole new set of jealousies. The spouse's sexual performances are often evaluated and give rise to the accusation, "You enjoyed it more than I did."

Another peculiar phenomenon is "dyadic jealousy." A couple may become jealous of another couple, and there are reports of overt demonstrations of jealous outbursts at parties which contrasts with the taboo on non-private displays of jealousy in the straight world.

Swinging dichotomizes male and female. While males may initiate swinging activity, females are frequently more adept because of the biological factors of sexuality and can perform more frequently. The accusation is frequently made, "Women have the best time at swinging," and, "Swinging is unfair to men."

Men who have been very confident about their sexuality frequently fail in the crucial moments of testing. This can deflate the male ego. Concentrating on improving his sexual experience can itself be self-defeating.

Fear of discovery—by straight neighbors, employees, fellow workers, relatives—hangs like the Sword of Damocles over the swinger's head.

While the secretive aspects of the swinger's life may provide much of the thrill in the early days, later on it becomes a subtle blackmail that keeps the swinger in a constant state of apprehension.

Deception lurks on every hand. In one of the letters to the editor of a swingers' magazine the correspondent complains about "the phonies who take advantage of people." The ads themselves contain phrases that give some indications of the problem: "no way outs," "no pros," "no hippies," "no dope users."

Operating in the swinging world is a chancy business.

Venereal disease is an ever-present hazard. Theoretically these respectable married couples should be safe, but, as we have already noted, female singles are often welcomed, and single males have a penchant for moving in. Some of these bring prostitutes with them, and so the potentiality is extended. When an outbreak of disease occurs, the suspect couple are reluctant to seek medical attention and fearful that a health department investigation may upset the group.

The homosexual angle gives ground for thought. Once the limits of sexuality are removed it sometimes moves in strange directions. The sex drive is remarkably malleable and, after all restrictions are off, can wander in some strange directions. The reports of women who may have been somewhat disillusioned by the male chauvinism in swinging discovering lesbian delights offers little ground for the belief that swinging may strengthen a marriage.

No matter what way you look at it, the swinger code that demands all participants be married is one fantastic almost unbelievable hypocrisy. To see the marriage certificate as a license for licentiousness is a horrendous travesty of marriage vows. The swinger with his smug assurance that only married people participate and no relationship should be allowed to develop is the hypocrite par excellence.

What of the family? The swinger's life may be one long series of deceptions as far as family life is concerned. Reports come of surreptitious phone calls that the children must not hear, pictures that must be carefully kept out of the children's reach, careful arrangements for baby sitters while parents swing, sending the children off to the in-laws' homes to clear the decks for a swinging party.

Dr. Auerback, a California psychiatrist, discusses the effect of swinging on children:

"In my clinical experience I have had the opportunity to see children brought up in a 'swinging household.' The parents, who had engaged in swinging for many years long before this practice was generally known or talked about, made no effort to conceal this from the children. In fact when the children were teenaged the parents encouraged their participation. One daughter ran away at the age of 15, quickly became pregnant and cut off further family contact. Another, at 17, left home to become a 'go-go' dancer. The oldest daughter, who consulted me for problems of frigidity, had reacted to the excessive sexual freedom in her home by becoming puritan in her behavior with consequent problems in marriage."⁵

We have already noted the exhibitionist tendencies of some swingers who take Polaroid pictures of their activities. The Polaroid has a measure of protection because the film doesn't have to be sent to a processor. But many of the swingers want to see the action, and so they take movies. The film is handed over to the processor who, while it is in his possession, can easily make a copy.

A report from the Chicago area tells of a twenty-one-year-old university student who went to a fraternity gathering to view some stag movies. He enjoyed the program tremendously until the third reel when to his embarrassment he saw his mother and father naked and involved in sex relations with another couple. The processor had made some extra money, but it was hardly the type of experience to strengthen home and family life.

We might ask ourselves the implications for a sensible view of sexuality. The most depressing single aspect of it all is that sex is reduced to a mere detached, mechanistic performance. The rule that you only swing once with a couple, the insistence that there be no terms of endearment, the lack of involvement, the absence of tenderness, the use of vibrators all insure that the all important elements of sexuality—commitment, affection, concern—are totally rejected.

Chapter Six

The Sad Inhabitants of the Gay World

The bearded minister stands facing the couple. He is offici-
ating at their wedding ceremony. They both carry flowers, on
the head of one is a garland, while the other has a neck encir-
cled with a similar wreath. The ceremony is brought to a conclusion as the minister says, "I pray God's blessing upon you
and the best of life for both of you." This might have been
just one of the numerous weddings that take place across the
United States in the classical nuptial month—the month of
June. One slight difference—both bride and groom are male—a
homosexual wedding.

Among the placards that have sprung with wild profusion in
protest against the establishment there has appeared one that
proclaims, "Gay is good." These militant homosexuals protest
in the streets, celebrate Gay Liberation Week, live in a commune called GLAD (Gay Liberation Arizona Desert), and attend churches where the preacher says of Jesus, "What would
you think of a man who never married and spent his days with
twelve other guys," and leads his congregation on protest
marches that embarrass more conservative homosexuals.

Carefully orchestrated as a background to these strident
voices is a subtle propaganda campaign. Many selling jobs
have been done with the American people, for after all we are
the nation of Madison Avenue, but few of these have ever
been done with either the skill or the success of the homosexual propagandists.

In part because many homosexuals move very naturally into
the entertainment world, they frequently have access to the
media with its unique opportunities to get across their ideas,

and they have not been slow to take advantage of the situation. In their strategic positions great numbers of homosexuals writers, actors, producers, and playwrights are zealously and with a sense of mission pushing their homophile philosophy.

A recent national television program had the homosexual theme, and at the conclusion many of the viewers paid a tribute to the skill of the propagandists when they remarked that it was "beautifully done." Therein lies its danger. With such acceptance more and more novels, movies, and plays are carrying the homosexual theme.

At a not so subtle level come the cheap pornographic books. These are frequently stories of heterosexuals, but they depict the "heteros" as gradually discovering the delights of the distinctive homosexual activities of fellatio, cunnilingus, and anal intercourse. Then the characters find the joy and convenience of a relationship with someone of their own sex who can provide all these types of sexual experiences without the demands that heteros lay on each other.

The artistic abilities, so frequently found among homosexuals, have not been allowed to go to waste, and great floods of visual material very explicit in its depictions of scenes and activity dear to the homosexual heart have been dropped upon the market.

One of these publications commences with a long spiel about the *Naturist Mind,* and having sounded this fashionable ecological note, claims it is a volume of pictures of people who not unnaturally call themselves nudists.

The high sounding phrases such as "naturists are very social in their outlook" and "nudism creates an atmosphere . . . in which men and women can communicate on a basic primal level not obtainable in the ordinary clothed society," may cause the interested reader to look for some evidence of socializing activities. But the pictures have no females. Men only. In pairs, with the phallus prominently displayed—only relieved by rear-end pictures with anal close ups. Judiciously mixed in here and there are some torture scenes typically showing one man holding the other aloft by a chain which brings the subject exquisite joy by biting into his groin.

As for the textual claim that the naturist's body and mind are formed by "most healthful exercises," they must utilize some new form of isometrics, for there is no sign of movement, only postures by males posed in such a way that they display every aspect of masculine anatomy.

The text itself is nothing more than fraudulent gobbledegook completely unrelated to serve only one purpose—to provide titillation for homosexual viewers. And, to cap it all, this skinny little book has a price tag of $4.00.

Society has always been much more tolerant of homosexual activity between women than among men. These women are generally referred to as lesbians, a word which comes originally from the Greek island Lesbos, the home of a notorious girls' school whose curriculum apparently included homosexual activities.

The pornographers have churned out a stream of lesbian material. A whole series of books abounding with pictures depict girls involved in lesbian activities. These are allegedly for the purpose of stimulating female homosexuals, but it is generally acknowledged that women are not as amenable to visual stimuli as are men, and the main market is really heterosexual males who often find some peculiar attraction to material displaying lusting females sexually stimulating each other.[1]

The Riddle of Inversion

What lies behind the riddle of homosexuality?

There are some theories about the way in which sexual development of an individual takes this turn. Some theorizers claim people are born this way. There seems to be little evidence for this point of view. Others claim the reason is the result of faulty relationships with one's parents in the early formative days.

There is another point of view that suggests that in some ways homosexuality is a learned behavior.

The development of the human personality is a complicated process, and the growing individual passes through a series of stages from birth to death. At one stage of childhood, a preoccupation with one's own sex is appropriate, but it normally leads at adolescence to a shift to a heterosexual object.

If in this stage the child is seduced and skillfully initiated by an experienced adult into homosexual activity, the child may be conditioned to this type of sexual response so that it becomes the preferred method of sexual expression.

At least partial confirmation for this theorizing has come

from the work of Masters and Johnson. Of 213 men whom they treated for sexual dysfunction, 21 had homosexual experiences as teenagers. Apparently the first initiatory sexual encounter was a significant factor. None of these men had engaged in heterosexual encounters before their homosexual activity.

The conclusion was, "The man whose first mature sexual experience is homosexual appears to be marked by it, even though he switches to heterosexual lovemaking. There may be some pattern imprinted on his behavior that cannot be erased. Both primarily and secondarily impotent men who had homosexual experiences as teenagers continued to think of themselves as homosexually oriented in their adult lives, even though many married."

Another researcher investigated the question as to whether homosexual desires or homosexual behavior came first. This investigator discovered that in a significant number of cases that he investigated his subjects had their first homosexual experiences before they were conscious of any homosexual desires and that another 12.3 percent of his subjects developed homosexual desires and homosexual behavior at about the same time. Significantly, in all the cases investigated by this researcher, 43 percent of the subjects had their first homosexual experiences before they were twelve years old.[2]

The frequent assertion that homosexuality is "natural" may need some qualifying. As opposed to animal life, human sexual behavior is much less the direct product of an instinctive drive, more flexible and pliable, and the outcome of learning experiences.

One researcher as we have noted in the previous chapter on swinging activities, discovered that homosexual activities between females is often a feature of these events. The lesbian activities were introduced at the behest of the men, and investigation showed something like two-thirds of the women who participated learned to enjoy lesbian activities. Some of them even went on to function exclusively as lesbians.

Urged on by their male tutors they had learned the lesson—learned it only too well—with the result that they turned aside from males whom they had reason to believe had used them badly, exploiting their lesbian activities for their own satisfaction.

Threat to Children

Any discussion of homosexuality is bound to reach a point where it focuses on the relationship of the invert to children. The Gay propagandists generally deny that this type of relationship has any significant part to play in their activities. However, when I found myself in the strange situation of giving a demonstration of counseling with a homosexual before a group of counselors, I asked, "What aged partners do you like best? Do the younger ones appeal to you?"

He answered, "Of course they do. In all sexuality, even heterosexuality, the younger sex objects are the more attractive."[3]

In Dallas, Texas, the police became interested in the activities of one particular man who had gathered a collection of some 700 pictures of nude males and females. Following up on complaints, it was discovered this individual was using his "gallery" as a means of luring juveniles into his home. At one time he had 25 juveniles with whom he had committed sodomy and whom he encouraged to engage in homosexual practices with each other.

Where do all these pictures come from?

In another Dallas case, three males had developed a circle of fifty juvenile boys whom they enticed to participate in homosexual activities while they were photographed. These pictures were then sold to distributors, and copies of them were traced to most states in the U. S. and abroad to Canada and Europe.[4]

Reports of this type of activity come from different parts of the U.S.A. One operation, described by *Time* magazine as "a homosexual ring that would fulfill the fantasies of Marquis de Sade," came to light in Nassau County, Long Island. Four adults were arrested in connection with "a national recruitment program of young boys for the purpose of deviant sexual conduct."[5]

The Nassau District Attorney revealed that the youngsters were "bribed with very expensive gifts, clothing, as were the families of the boys. It was inferred that the recruiters were members of the Big Brother movement, since most of the boys were fatherless."

These boys ranging in age from as young as seven years were brought from all over the U.S., Canada, Mexico, and

Puerto Rico, were seduced and trained in homosexual techniques.

Significantly, investigation revealed that few of the boys had any propensity for homosexual conduct before they met up with these men and that most of them objected and had to be bribed or threatened before they finally consented to participate.

The Proselytizing Religion

The big news in homosexual circles in recent days has been the development of a series of so-called Community Churches which are ministered to by a homosexual minister and have a Gay membership.

At the head of this movement stands a young man who is a graduate of a conservative Bible school. He had his first homosexual experience at nine years of age but did not "come out" and acknowledge his homosexuality until he was 23 years old.

Functioning at this time as a minister of a denominational church, he separated from his wife and church and decided to "go west" where he established the new church referred to at this time as the Sodomy Church.

Interestingly enough, homosexuality itself is sometimes referred to as a "proselytizing religion," not so much because of its religion but rather the enthusiasm with which it carries on its proselytizing.

Dick Leitsch, the director of the Homosexual Mattachine Society, in an interview discussed homosexual activity, "Men in our society are taught promiscuity is a good thing—the Playboy ideal, you know, love 'em and leave 'em when you get next month's Bunny. Male homosexuals are like this. We have sex as often as possible to prove to ourselves that we're men because men are supposed to have a lot of sex."[6]

What's Wrong with Inversion?

There are many unsatisfactory aspects of the invert's way of life which would include the following:

*The Bible says the practice is wrong, and for a professing Christian there will always be a haunting uncertainty.

*It is, particularly with the male, sex without relationship. Everything focuses on the orgastic moment.

*When two inverts set up a relationship of living together the pathway is generally one of distrust and jealousy.

*The constant prowl of many homosexuals looking for new conquests with straight people and the tendency to turn to younger sex objects makes the demand for sexual relationships between "consenting adults" meaningless.

*Far from being the gentle, kind, loving people as they are frequently portrayed, many of the members and associates of the gay world are sadistic and take advantages of each other.

*Growing old presents a problem. As one ex-homosexual says it, "The elderly homosexual is a pathetic sight, particularly the one who has no money. He begs for handouts. He will give a man a blow job then ask for a dollar, fifty cents, or even a quarter. This is the way he will make money to buy his wine. As the years go by loneliness becomes a greater problem."[7]

*Venereal disease is a real hazard. Evelyn Hooker speaks about homosexuality and refers to the "frantic promiscuity" of the Los Angeles homosexual community. An investigator with the San Francisco Bay City Clinic says it is not unusual for some homosexuals to have as many as fifty or sixty contacts a month, and all of this has taken its toll. In the midst of a rising tide of venereal disease which is reaching epidemic proportions, investigators in the San Francisco area have reported that up to forty per cent of new cases of syphilis occur among male homosexuals.

*One homosexual confessed that he had never actually enjoyed the sexual experiences. It was rather the mystique of it all, the fear of getting caught, belonging to an illicit group that gave him a thrill.

*Homosexuality is sometimes a manifestation of an underlying maladjustment. Cappon, who has written at length on homosexuality says, "The homosexual person at best, will be unhappier and more unfulfilled than the sexually normal person . . . The natural history of the homosexual person seems to be one of frigidity, impotence, broken personal relationships, psychosomatic disorders, alcoholism, paranoid psychosis (i.e., the mental illness of suspicion and persecution) and suicide."[8]

A very frank appraisal of homosexuality has come from an unlikely source. After former Teamsters President James Hoffa had been released from penitentiary he became an enthusiastic advocate of prison reform. Having had a chance during his five years in federal penitentiary to observe the homosexual practices of a number of the inmates he complained about the guards who condoned the homosexual practices of prisoners, ". . . allowing any two people that want to live together to move into a common joint cell. And they think it's cute to have them walking up and down, swishing around holding hands . . . . But they likewise know that it endangers every inmate in that prison because of the possibility of a riot over homosexuality." Hoffa added, "It is a terrible problem. It creates stabbings, fights, riots."[9]

Apparently the free and open practice of homosexuality didn't bring a millennium to a penitentiary, but it may serve as a warning as to what can happen when homosexuality is legitimized in a social setting.

Although many homosexuals put on a front and widely advertise that they are satisfied and happy in their way of life, one survey showed that only two per cent of them would want their son to be a homosexual.

Gay people are the most unsure people ever. They are not really gay. They are sad, sad, sad.

As one man has said, "Show me a gay homosexual, and I'll show you a Gay corpse."

Chapter Seven

Depersonalized Sex

Walt Disney and Masters and Johnson teamed up in a new enterprise?

It seems like an improbable alliance, but many people see this as a possible combination that helped to spawn a whole flood of products that have inundated the pornographic marketplace.

Of course Walt Disney—blessings be upon him for furnishing so much family entertainment—made his contribution unwittingly as he developed a technique by which he could create a realistic Abraham Lincoln to deliver again some of his immortal utterances, or a gleaming-skinned native who would leap out spear in hand to thrill a child during the Disneyland African river cruise. These figures where so lifelike and convincing that many inventive minds quickly envisaged a much wider application of the modelling skill.

Masters and Johnson, with serious scientific intent, were developing some remarkable equipment for the laboratories, where they carried out scientific research that used a wide variety of esoteric instruments for sexually stimulating, observing, and recording the reactions of the subjects for this sophisticated sexual investigation. The nature of their work and the innovative methods they used suggested possibilities to many an observer with an eye for a fast buck.

Most of us have been able to take the technological developments of a space age in our stride, and though we have only a limited understanding of what is going on, we accept the marvels of all this scientific progress and gradually become quite casual about such a remarkable feat as astronauts landing on the moon. Despite all this, it comes with something of a jolt to discover that modern technology has moved in on the most intimate experiences of man—his sexual reactions.

Although rather crude sexual accessories have been around for many a year, one of the "spin offs" of the new advances in technology may be a remarkable sophistication in what has been called, "Those groovy bedroom sex gadgets." Although it is still in its infancy, the sex gadget industry is nevertheless doing a multi-million dollar business annually.

This is just a beginning. The designers have gone back to their drawing boards and have projected such mind boggling ideas as a thoroughly mechanized bordello staffed with robots which would in the words of one authority be ". . . better than the real thing, more beautiful than call girls, more eager to please, untiring and perhaps capable of more impossible contortions."

Perhaps the ultimate in sex gadgets may be in the offing. "One day, perhaps inside of twenty years, it will be feasible to feed into the brain, electrically, not just pleasure or excitement (that can already be done), but a whole sex fantasy, a real-life movie with sight, sound, taste, touch and smell. The society that might want such a thing has been described in, [an imaginative book] in which men and women immerse themselves in body-temperature baths [to cut off external sensation], blindfold themselves and don skull caps with electrodes that feed in a "sex tape" carrying the chosen perversion or sex scene. To the wearer of the skull cap, the experience is as real as real-life, but he is transformed into a man with superhuman powers (or, for women, into a girl of incredible beauty, and so on) . . . Machines already able to perform most human functions more efficiently than humans, are one day going to be able to have sex better than we can, in a manner of speaking."[1]

But even today we have some fairly complex sexual gadgets, and if a Martian were to arrive on our globe from outerspace and chance to wander into one of the "porno shops" presently dotting the landscape, he would probably wonder at the technological sophistication of earthlings, and conclude that for them sexual experiences were akin to surgical procedures, and marvel at the whole array of instrumentation they apparently used.

Should you follow the Martian example and wander into a

"porno shop," your first impression would probably be of the strange pall of silence on the place which makes this sex shop resemble a mausoleum. It may be a tacit acknowledgement that this is a place of lifeless bodies, bereft of every lofty impulse that might be indicative of life, and embalmed to keep them available for visitors whose only interest lies in the sexual aspects of life.

Along with the usual displays of books and magazines, many of them carefully wrapped in cellophane to impede the free-lookers, are shelves with sexual gadgets of all sorts and sizes.

Included in these displays are dildoes, some elaborately constructed of rubber and plastic, in choice of colors, and so built that they can ejaculate when a bulb is pressed. The vibrator, once the favored instrument for reducing muscle soreness or smoothing away unwanted pains, has now been adapted to the sexual field as the preeminent instrument for masturbation with special types built for male or female usage.

Special dolls variously called love dolls, party dolls, or fornication dolls represent the ultimate in gadgetry. These are, in the words of an ad, "Life size, 5'4" tall, 37"-23"-36", completely life-like in every detail, a young body you'll love to touch. Add air and it is ready for action—your perfect playmate."

These products grow more sophisticated. News comes of one doll that has a system that can be heated with warm water to achieve the correct body temperature and a mechanism that will cause genital contractions to give the impression that it is experiencing orgasm.

To complete these pornographic Barbi Dolls, the owner can purchase special kits of sexually tantalizing clothes. One supplier, appropriately named "The Undie World," advertises "Sensuous Set—black leather—Zippie two piece bra and mini-skirt so sexy it sizzles." Along with these go bikinis, wigs, panties, bras, and peek-a-boo negligees. All are available in the black color, which is seen by some as being particularly sexy, but one doesn't have to be a Freudian psychologist to see a symbolism of the dearth of live feminine participation in this type of sex.

Among these autoerotic devices comes the inevitable homosexual angle. Preeminently advertised in many of the porno-publications are the rectal vibrators which according to the ads, are inserted into the rectum for sexual stimulation.

With burgeoning discount houses springing up to supply homes with appliances so dear to feminine hearts, frost-free refrigerators, radar ranges, spraying irons, blower hair dryers, it naturally follows that the manufacturers of sexual appliances should develop some of the same marketing techniques that had been so successful with the more mundane domestic appurtenances. A visitor to Germany soon discovers, what are sometimes referred to as "Sex Supermarkets," where every sexual device that could be imagined, and many beyond the capacity of most imaginative people, are to be found.

In the world of pornography masturbation has achieved a new and lofty status. The practice has come a long way since the days when it was referred to as the "heinous sin of self-pollution" and said to be dangerous, draining off the masturbator's strength, or would finally send him to what was then called the insane asylum. Taking advantage of a new turn in the tide of opinion, a whole group of authorities have appeared with a new liberated idea that, not only is masturbation not dangerous, but it is a very natural activity that provides a sex outlet which is beneficial for the individual.[2]

Take the case of "J".

By her own admission she is a singularly unattractive gal with heavy thighs, bumpy hips, protruding teeth, a ski jump nose, poor posture, flat feet, and uneven ears. Though with a figure like this it would probably have been rather futile, she admits she doesn't wear tight skirts, low cut dresses, or bikinis, and, she further confesses, she has little of the personality appeal that so often attracts men.

Yet despite all these debits one experience changed this Plain Jane's whole style of life and made her into a much sought after companion, friend, and lover. Since that devastating moment of revelation some of the most interesting men in America have fallen in love with her. She claims she had proposals for marriage from a concert pianist, a best selling author, the producer of three of America's most popular television shows, a bomb expert for the Central Intelligence Agency, a trial attorney, an apple grower, a TV and radio star, and a tax expert.

How did all this happen?

Well—she suddenly discovered she had the wrong idea—she had been laboring under an illusion. She didn't really know what men wanted, and she had been using the wrong bait to

Open Flood Gates

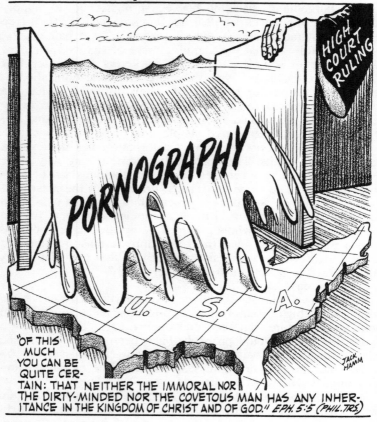

"OF THIS MUCH YOU CAN BE QUITE CERTAIN: THAT NEITHER THE IMMORAL NOR THE DIRTY-MINDED NOR THE COVETOUS MAN HAS ANY INHERITANCE IN THE KINGDOM OF CHRIST AND OF GOD." EPH. 5:5 (PHIL. TRS.)

lure them into the sphere of her influence.

She foolishly—so she says—used to imagine that men wanted good-looking wives, gals bubbling over with effervescent personalities, a woman who would be a good housekeeper and manager of the family finances, and a wife who would be a good mother to raise his children.

Now she has discovered she was wrong wrong, wrong. That is *not* what men want. What they really want is—get this—a

DANGEROUS SPARRING PARTNER

"ABSTAIN FROM FLESHLY LUSTS, WHICH WAR AGAINST THE SOUL"
— I PET. 2:11

sensuous woman. Let a gal develop some sexual techniques, and she can be as ugly as sin, absolutely bereft of personality, a slob around the house, have no interest in home and family, but let her actualize her potential sensuality, and all these extraneous and superficial things matter nothing at all.

This cornball version of the old commercial, "They all laughed but when I sat down to play . . . ," is another of the pieces of pornography which skyrocketed on to the best seller list as women, taken in by a shrewd advertising campaign, sought to discover how it was that such a plain homely girl, with no personality could accomplish all this by just learning the secrets of being a good performer in bed.

As this particular volume is a "do-it-yourself" manual, it introduces the subject to the secrets of sensuality with a series of "setting up" exercises that lead to the heart of it all. The key that really opens the door to all sensuality is masturbation. As she says it, "Smart women masturbate quite a lot, because they have discovered that it opens the doors of sensuality to them for it strengthens and increases the flexibility of the love muscles, helps the body to coordinate fully at demand, and teaches women to have orgasms—many orgasms—easily." To the unsophisticated reader it now becomes clear that the "open sesame" to all these sexual delights is the discovery and development of sophisticated techniques of sexual self-stimulation.

A similar manual for men makes the same general approach. The advantages of autoeroticism include such factors as simplicity, convenience, and economy which lead to the unmined lode of sensual delight.

If these masturbation skills are to be practiced at the rate suggested by the publications, there must be some aphrodisiac, and the pornographers are standing by and ready to help. Probably the main use of most pornographic literature is to provide titillation for masturbation. This can take many different forms. One of the masturbation guidebooks not only suggests techniques but guides the practitioner toward certain books of erotic stories that will help to sexually stimulate and support him in his activities.

The same is true of X-rated movies, where many of the viewers masturbate as they watch, and some of the strip-tease shows, where strippers report with a derisive note in their voice that a number of the spectators are masturbating during the presentation.

An Evaluation of Autoeroticism

One perceptive observer has lamented, "The sexual pleasure one gets from pornography and obscenity is autoerotic and infantile, put bluntly it is a masturbatory exercise of the imagination, when it is not masturbation pure and simple,[3] and because masturbation stands at the heart of the world of

COSTLY RESTRAINT

pornography we need to examine the whole concept of auto-eroticism.

The old, widely held view was that sexual self-stimulation was a dangerous practice that would wreck havoc on the masturbator, possibly leaving him physically, if not psychologically, damaged. Few people would really try to maintain this position today.

A second approach to the subject is that of the pornographic

CONTINUUM FOR EVALUATING AUTOEROTICISM

ACCEPTABLE				*UNDESIRABLE*
BABYHOOD	CHILDHOOD	ADOLESCENCE	SINGLE	MARRIED
Dawning sensory awareness— Accidental contact	Introduction by peers— Observing others	New sexual awareness— Tension— Uncertainty of sexual role	Unmarried— Widowed— Separated from spouse	Heterosexual outlet available—Auto-eroticism gesture of defiance

world, which feeds on masturbation and must do anything it can to support the practice. From this point of view masturbation is not only natural but perfectly healthy and in fact, highly desirable.

A third approach to this subject indicates that any consideration of masturbation must take a number of factors into consideration and suggests the criterion, "At what stage of development and under what circumstances?"

For the purposes of evaluation, the experience may be plotted on the continuum as indicated in the accompanying chart.

From this perspective all of life is a constantly unfolding process of which sexuality is only one, albeit a very important, part. Autoerotic activities may be observed even in baby days when the infant makes accidental contact with its genitals and from experience of pleasure continues the practice.

Adolescence, the watershed between childhood and adulthood, is a period when masturbation may be both the symbol of infantile sexuality and the foretaste of a more satisfying coitus experience. The situation is complicated still further because the adolescent is physically capable of sexual congress even though somewhat uncertain about his ability, but has not reached the standard of educational, vocational, or social functioning that will enable him to take on marital responsibilities. Masturbation may provide a release from tension and even seem virtuous as it saves the subject from violating prohibitions against premarital sexual relations.

The word "single" on the chart needs some interpretation. It encompasses a whole wide category of people. People looking toward marriage—those who for various reasons have never married—a great number who because of death, divorce or defection are on their own—individuals separated from spouses either geographically or because of illness are all gathered under this category.

From this perspective any evaluation of masturbation is made against the continuum form "acceptable" to undesirable." Masturbation in babies and children will be viewed with tolerance, if not ease; in adolescence understanding, as, too, in a single experience. The crisis point comes when, as in marriage, heterosexual experiences are available, but masturbation continues to be the preferred sexual outlet.

As an end sexual experience in itself masturbation has some very unsatisfactory aspects.

Preeminently, masturbation is an elemental sexual reaction and is the simplest physiological technique of inducing orgasm. If orgasm is all that is sought in sexual reaction apart from closeness or personality interaction, masturbation may provide the simple means of attainment.

Autoerotic practices characteristically involve a fantasy element which may itself bring problems. Masters and Johnson suggest a possibility in reply to a question concerning female autoeroticism.

"Fantasies facilitate self-stimulation. If these are consistently devoted to unattainable goals (a movie-star lover, for instance) or to unacceptable practices (being raped or, the other side of the coin, torturing the male), they lead the woman away from the goal of successful union with the man of her choice."[4]

Possibly the greatest single deficiency in sexual self-stimulation is that the practice by-passes the elements of affiliation and relatedness. One of the joys of a sexual encounter is the response of a partner. The solitary sexual experience in masturbation misses this significant aspect of human sexuality.

All the worrying we've done over the dangers of guilt arising from masturbation may not be as necessary as we formerly thought. Ideally, guilt is a positive force pushing us to achieve our potential. This same force, in a gentle nudging fashion, may be needed to ease us away from infantile sexuality toward a full mature heterosexuality.

The guilt engendered by exposure to certain sexually explicit publications, films, art work may serve a similar purpose to help us move beyond the preoccupations with depersonalized sex characteristic of a pornography described by one authority as, "a masturbatory fantasy."

Chapter Eight

The Two Million Dollar Boondoggle

As the set of books repose on the shelf they look quite attractive in a sparse sort of way. Buff-colored covers with black title on the spine give the impression of economy in production. The only hint of color is in the end papers, blue, and bearing the title *Technical Report of the Commission on Obscenity and Pornography,* plus volume number and the subject, "The Market Place," "Legal Analysis," "The Consumer and The Community," "Erotica and Anti-Social Behavior"—and so on through the ten volumes.

Some alert citizens wonder if the set shouldn't have red leather covers with embossed gold lettering and be printed on parchment, with cloth of gold tassels, for that little set of books cost two million dollars.

Not for a buyer mind you. A prospective purchaser can obtain them for about $20.00 from the Printing Office which is a bargain, but the U. S. Superintendent of Documents has always been a very generous fellow, who believes it is better to let you make an indirect payment through your tax dollar, rather than require you to put the money down on the counter.

The path of the Commission had been carefully charted. The two most influential men, the Chairman and the Legal Counsel, were both committed to a philosophy that any effort to control pornography was undesirable. And on this basis the structure of the Commission and its staff fell into place.

Congress had assigned four specific tasks to the Commission:

(1) with the aid of leading constitutional law authorities, to analyze the laws pertaining to the control of obscenity and pornography; and to evaluate and recommend definitions of obscenity and pornography;

97

(2) to ascertain the methods employed in the distribution of obscene and pornographic materials and to explore the nature and volume of traffic in such materials;

(3) to study the effect of obscenity and pornography upon the public, and particularly minors, and its relationship to crime and other antisocial behavior; and

(4) to recommend such legislative, administrative, or other advisable and appropriate action as the Commission deems necessary to regulate effectively the flow of such traffic, without in any way interfering with constitutional rights.

To most people this would seem to be a fairly clear mandate that would involve some relatively simple procedures but the Commission went at its task in a manner that seemed to indicate it had grave doubts about its own ability to fulfill its function and found it necessary to pass over its responsibility to others.

While it is possible to study drug abuse without ever having experimented with drugs, or to look into the problems of alcoholism without imbibing liquor, it is highly improbable that anyone can ever know anything about pornography without having examined the material. Much of this is so far out, that even seasoned investigators find themselves set back by the blatancy of it all. Yet this Commission, with such an awesome responsibility to make recommendations with regard to national policy, dealt with the broad subject of pornography at second hand. Dissenting members claimed that, "Commissioners themselves were not put into direct contact with the problem of obscenity in the concrete. A few films were shown at the first meeting; samples were 'available,' but no Commissioner was asked to become conversant with the problem in the concrete, so that he could be equipped to make judgments."[1]

When the report ultimately appeared it encouraged the pornographers tremendously. The conclusions of the Commission made it sound as if an enormous paranoia must have descended upon the citizens of the United States causing them to imagine that some sinister force was at work undermining their society. Congress had apparently been caught up in this unreasonable hysteria and had declared, "pornography is a matter of national concern," whereas in reality, so the Commission claimed, there was absolutely no danger and if everybody had just ignored the whole matter it would have gone away.

The Commission concluded that instead of some nationwide

movement to distribute pornography it was simply a spasmodic effort of small proportions, the influence of the material on anybody's mind, either young or old, was negligible, and laws against pornography were futile and unnecessary. They grudgingly acknowledged that pornography might be inappropriate for the young. Consequently, the only type of legislation necessary was that which had to do with "a range of explicit pictorial and three dimensional depictions of sexual activity. It does not apply to depictions of nudity alone . . . "[2] So came a recommendation of token legislation on public display and invasion of privacy through the mails.

However, even in this decision there was a difference. Two members of the Commission expressed their dismay at this proposed legislation. These two members stated unequivocally that no laws of any type that limited pornography were required.

A stunned general public pinched itself to see if it were awake. And forthwith came a whole series of indignant reactions.

Co-publisher and editor of the *Dallas Times Herald*, Felix R. McKnight, "Hogwash."

Postmaster General Winton H. Blount pointed out that the Commission's findings "are not conclusive, and they should not be construed as though they are."

Representative John H. Murphy called for a Congressional investigation on the ground that the Commission had "wasted almost $2 million of the taxpayer's money to produce an erroneous and harmful report."

The Senate passed a resolution by 60 votes to five which said in part, "The Senate declares that (1) generally the findings and recommendations are not supported by the evidence considered by or available to the Commission and (2) the Commission has not properly performed its duties nor has it complied with the mandates of Congress."

President Nixon reacted with an uncharacteristically harsh judgment, "The Commission has performed a disservice and I totally reject its report."

It wasn't just politicians and columnists. Among behavioral scientists none stand higher than the remarkable husband and wife team of Sheldon and Eleanor Glueck. Authors of sixteen volumes including their unique Prediction Tables for forecasting potential delinquents and criminals, they have been widely acclaimed as leaders in the field. Asked by a reporter if pornography were harmful, Dr. Glueck had a forthright response:

That was the question before the President's Commission on Obscenity and Pornography, a majority of the commission concluded that it found no evidence that exposure to, or use of explicit sexual material is harmful—for example, in causing delinquent or criminal behavior among youth or adults.

However, I question the soundness of some of the research methods by which the Commission drew its inferences and conclusions. The very fact that Federal and State statutes controlling dissemination of pornographic and obscene materials have long been on the books, creates a strong presumption that the people find such materials harmful.

The Commission itself admits that its information is incomplete and many of its findings are tentative. Yet it does not hesitate to recommend the removal of legislation prohibiting the dissemination of pornographic and obscene materials.

It does seem obvious that much more exploration is needed of the effects of pornographic materials, especially on children—not a naive attempt to find a point-to-point connection between exposure to pornography and sexual or other crimes. Our own investigations have shown the causes of anti-social behavior to be extremely complex. It is futile to pull out one factor from many and define it as *the* cause of such behavior. What is really involved is not just sexual crime or delinquency but the question of pornography's impact on various aspects of human life, and especially on the general moral climate.[3]

The proud boast of the Commission was that it had taken a scientific stance and reached its conclusions on the basis of empirical studies carried out by them or on their behalf. From the outset they rejected the idea that opinions of people, no matter how authoritative they might be, were of any importance. Only two hearings were held and these took place because the dissenters had forced them into such a procedure. Yet, in at least one of their determinations they placed credence in opinions.

On the basis of opinions the Commission decided, among other things, that Americans were not concerned about pornography as a national problem. In a survey conducted on behalf of the Commission people were asked, "Would you please tell me what you think are the two or three most serious problems in America today?"

Answering this question, only two percent of the people polled stated that they thought pornography was a major problem, and from these responses the pollsters decided Americans were not really concerned about pornography.

If the Commission were seriously interested in the business of opinion polls it might have been a good idea to compare its results with those of some highly respected pollsters who conducted their investigation in about the same time period.

The following were the results of polls taken in the years 1969-70:

Harris Poll (1969): 76 per cent of U. S. wants pornography outlawed.

Gallup Poll (1969): 85 per cent of the U. S. favor stricter laws on pornography.

Abelson (1970): 2 per cent of the U. S. viewed pornography as a serious national problem (a Commission study).

The Commission was prepared to accept the results of a poorly devised and administered poll while at the same time ignoring some of the more valid efforts of widely experienced workers in the field.

Pornographers have always had a tendency to tell the whole story. It's not what they tell, but what they don't tell, that causes the problem. Apparently the Commission was, in its judgment of pornography, guilty of using at least one of the pornographer's methods.

A glaring example of this was seen in the treatment of the Davis-Brauch report. This report had to do with a study of 365 people from seven different groups and sought to discover the relationship between exposure to pornography and moral character.

At the time when this research was completed some information about its findings leaked out and several newspapers carried stories of the way in which the study indicated a relationship between exposure to pornography and sex deviance.

One member of the Commission notes that this report was never shared with the members of that body, and when the final report of the Commission was released, it failed to mention these particular findings.

Davis and Brauch, whose research methodology and statistical treatment was particularly impressive stated:

" 'One finds exposure to pornography is the strongest predictor of sexual deviance among the early age of exposure subjects.'[4] Later they again note, 'In general, then, exposure to pornography in the 'early age of exposure' subgroup was related to a variety of precocious, heterosexual and deviant sexual behaviors.' "[5]

In the preface of the technical report on *The Impact of Erotica* the Commission's statement reads, "If a case is to be made against 'pornography' in 1970, it will have to be made on grounds other than demonstrated effects of a damaging personal or social nature. Empirical research designed to clarify the question has found no reliable evidence to date that exposure to explicit sexual materials plays a significant role in the causation of delinquent or criminal sexual behavior among youth or adults."[6]

"Empirical research."

This statement, cited over again and again through the report is made with an easy confidence that assumes the last word has been said.

We have already noted Glueck's dissatisfaction with the simplistic approach of the research which ignored the complex factors involved and characterized the Commission's efforts as, " . . . the naive attempt a point-to-point connection between exposure to pornography and sexual and other crimes." But even the research on these "point-to-point connections," is very much under question as to the conclusions drawn from the research data.

Dr. Victor B. Cline, psychologist and specialist in social science methodology, has carefully examined the information available on the research conducted by the staff members of the Commission and concludes it is *"seriously flawed and omitting some critical data on negative effects."*[7]

When this behavioral scientist appeared before the Commission in Los Angeles he made a request that no reputable social scientist could reasonably decline. He asked that a panel of scientists be set up to: (a) evaluate the original research sponsored by the Commission, (b) assess what conclusions might legitimately be drawn from the assembled evidence.[8]

In his final evaluation, Dr. Cline took the studies one at a time and ferreted out a great number of deficiencies in both the design of the research and the conclusions reached.

Cline came up with some caustic comments and rebuttals. He strongly disputed the conclusions that the purchasers of erotica are well-educated, middle-class males in their 30's and 40's, that sex offenders come from conservative, repressed sexually-deprived backgrounds, that pornography doesn't change behavior, that sex crimes are not related to pornography, and that people get satiated through exposure to pornography. In each of these areas he produced evidences of faulty research, and, or, erroneous conclusions in the work of the Commission's staff.

Second Thoughts

After spending two million dollars in money and two years of time the President's Commission has left many Americans disappointed if not disillusioned.

Perhaps we can take courage from the experience from the Earl of Longford. This British peer of the realm is a life-long socialist who calls himself a "fellow travelling member of Women's Lib" and was the first member of the House of Lords to come out in favor of legalizing private adult homosexual acts. Then the socialist lord went to a London theatre, an institution not known of recent days for puritanical performances, and saw the production of "Oh! Calcutta!" The experience so impressed the Lord that he hastened to the House of Lords where he delivered an anti-obscenity speech and launched an investigation into the influences of pornography.

After 16 months of research during which time the committee sampled all the wide varieties of the pornographers' art, interviewed purveyors of literature, witnessed performers on the stage, held discussions with policemen, and read some 5,000 letters that poured into the committee. This 52 man committee, consisting of bishops, social scientists, housewives, educators, pop stars, and writers, produced a 520 page report on pornography and reached the conclusion that pornography creates an addiction leading to deviant obsessions and actions.

Their recommendation—Britain's anti-obscenity laws be strengthened and extended.

Unscientific?

After America's experience with commissioners who had little personal contact with pornography and employed a staff of experts to do the direct work, operated with secrecy, only reluctantly conducted a couple of hearings, and came up with a sadly flawed product, it is refreshing to find a broad-based report that at least reflects the common sense of many ordinary people.

The Logical Response

Immediately upon the publication of the Commission's report on obscenity and pornography a couple of significant publications appeared.

One, entitled *Porno and Obscenity,* has the sub-title, "A Pictorial Study of the Report of the President's Commission."

The text, such as it is, draws a number of unwarranted conclusions, but it is the pictorial element which really puts the icing on the cake.

In the style that cheap pornography has developed, the illustrations have no real relationship to the text. Plate #1 sets the tone with illustrations of dildoes for both rectal and vaginal use, then comes a portfolio of erotica, an ancient masturbating machine for women, a whole series of pictures of women performing fellatio, including one with semen on the woman's face. Along with this are explicit depictions of cunnilingus involving black and white men engaged in intercourse, and beastiality involving women and dogs.

But the worst feature is the pictorial representations of sadism and masochism. Pictures of men whipping women's buttocks, women tied in chains, a woman bound and gagged with a metal clamp on her nose while a man with pliers squeezes the nipple of her breast. Another depicts a woman bound and gagged while someone fastens a pair of pliers on her clitoris.

While no one in his right mind would blame the Presidential report for these activities, it is obvious that the publishers of this type of literature felt they now had a manifesto and went ahead with their cheap perverted smut.

But the edition to end all editions is titled *The Illustrated Presidential Report of the Commission on Obsenity and Pornography,* thumbing its nose at other weaker efforts like the *Pictorial Study,* notes it is *The Complete Text* and includes an introductory preface by the Executive Director for Southern California of the American Civil Liberties Union urging that people read the report and "support its recommendation and see to it that they are brought to pass."

Foolish Liberation

The illustrations of this volume are alleged to be pictorial commentaries on the text but in actual fact are examples of some of the most depraved forms of sexual activity that could be imagined. The compilers had apparently searched back into history and around the world to assemble their inane collection.

On the pretext that reference is made in the text of the Commission's report to Denmark a whole flood of pictures of

Danish pornography are reproduced. One display is acknowledged as coming from the Danish publication *Erotisk Tyang* (literally "enforced sex!"). Pictures in this series show men chained up with phallus bound with thin rope, a woman suspended by her arms, with chains around her body while men force a dildo into her. The Danish theme is further used to make a big display of human animal sex showing women involved in sexual activity with a pig, a donkey, a horse and a bull. But the daddy of them all is a picture of an eight-year-old girl sitting in an upright position while having intercourse with a mature man. This horrendous piece of pornography sold for $12.50 a copy.

Speaking at the American Psychopathological Association Dr. Morris Lipton, a member of the Commission, said, "It is a travesty of our serious efforts," but the Commission staff seems to have had other ideas.

A Federal Jury in San Diego convicted four men on eleven counts of mailing obscene advertisements. The case involved promotional material for *The Illustrated Report of the Commission on Obscenity and Pornography* and the book itself. During the trial W. Cody Wilson, Executive Director of the Presidential Commission, testified that the volume with the 300 hardcore pornographic pictures had "social redeeming value."

The very fact that a man who had occupied such a high position in the Commission could have testified that this unadulterated smut had "socially redeeming value" either indicates the prostitution of the English language or helps us to understand the reason why the Commission on Obscenity and Pornography reached the strange conclusions that it did.

No country has ever launched such an expensive and allegedly thorough investigation into pornography as did the United States in this instance. Of the activities of the Commission it may be said as it was in another connection—it goes down deeper, stays down longer, and comes up dirtier than any other effort.

Chapter Nine

Therapeutic or Corrupting?

One little-known incident of World War II has recently come to light and provides an interesting sidelight on the uses of pornography. Allied intelligence agents had uncovered some little-known information on the personality of Adolf Hitler. From this intelligence it became clear that Hitler was a sexual deviate. Starting from this premise the U. S. Office of Strategic Services (OSS) came up with a recommendation that the Allies use their information and exploit the dictator's weakness.

The plan was the essence of simplicity. Photographers would be commissioned to produce some particularly good examples of erotic pictures. This material would be air dropped into the grounds of Hitler's residence. It was hoped that as the dictator wandered around the grounds of his home he'd stumble upon the packet—marked "Erotic pictures for adults only?"—and open it. Upon perusing the contents the Fuehrer would be overwhelmed by the pornographic pictures.

This mind already in a state of disequilibrium would lose its balance and capitulate to the pressures. The men in white coats would carry him off to the psychiatric hospital and leave the Axis powers with a drooling sex maniac as their leader and thus bring about an inevitable collapse.

Looking back on this plan from the perspective of our day, there are many contemporary experts in the field of human sexuality who feel that not only would this plan, if carried out, have failed to hurt Adolf Hitler, but it would probably have had a positive therapeutic effect upon him. According to this reasoning such a diet of pornography might have been just what a man with a sexual hang-up really needed to help him handle his neurotic reactions. Thus the plan may have backfired, and given Germany a new confident leader, free from those neurotic obstacles that had haunted him for so long.

Is pornography therapeutic or corrupting, a curse or a blessing, a hindrance or a help?

Trying to look at the situation with at least a modicum of impartiality, demands that we consider some of the arguments for and against pornography. These include:

1. The Satiation Theory
2. The Catharsis Concept
3. The Denmark Argument
4. The Education Pitch
5. The No Effect Contention

The Satiation Theory

A simple statement of the conclusion of the President's Commission on Obscenity and Pornography would be that the sexual appetite is fairly easily satiated. While pornography may make its initial appeal, if a person is constantly exposed to sexual stimulation, the appetite will become jaded and the subject will soon lose interest in this sort of material.

Following this line of reasoning the answer to the problems of pornography is simple. The material is more of a nuisance than a menace, to ban it is a bad case of over-kill that only makes the prohibited more desirable. Just turn loose all the restrictions on pornography, and though there may be a temporary avalanche of the stuff, once the novelty has worn off, people will lose interest in what is no longer forbidden fruit, and the situation will take care of itself.

One basis for this type of conclusion was an experimental study carried out on behalf of the Commission. In this study twenty-three college men served as subjects and were exposed to the stimulus of pornography in a setting which was described, "removing all clothing and putting on a loose robe, hooking up one's penis to a condom and electrodes, attaching electrical instruments to both ears, putting a bellows around one's chest, being observed through a one-way window and sitting in an "isolation booth" for one and a half hours a day for fifteen days."[1]

By measuring the reactions of the subjects the experimenters concluded that exposure to pornography had a diminishing effect on the subjects.

In consideration of the inferences drawn from this study we might ask ourselves if this was really a good way to discover the effect of pornography. These college men paid to do the job, fitted out like astronauts about to depart for outer space, in a laboratory setting, were in an entirely different situation from that of an individual secluded in the privacy of his own room poring over erotic material.

Moreover this experiment ran for a limited 15 days, and completely overlooked the factor of *periodicity* in sexual response. Sex, like hunger, is a *recurring appetite*. It does not continue for long periods of time at the same level. Sexual excitation typically moves to peaks of desire, then release, which may give place to temporary loss of interest to be followed later by a new buildup of response.

It has long been noted that a man may be stimulated by his partner's nude body across the years, and he will pass through the cycle of stimulation, orgasm, satiation, then after a period of time a repetition of the whole cycle of experience. As physician John Cavanaugh puts it, "It is generally recognized that the sex appetite and interest is one of the most quickly satiated but also one of the most likely to return."

Strangely enough there were some Commission studies that indicated that among the patrons of pornographic bookstores and dirty movies, 52% of the people observed were regular customers. Another of the studies carried out in San Francisco indicated that 70% of the patrons of the sex movies attend at least once a month. The study showed that 49% of these people were involved in sexual experiences with two or more partners at this time. The correlation of high exposure to pornography and high intercourse frequency hardly suggests satiation.

Commenting on the fact that many men continued to purchase erotica, the President's Commission's report reached the remarkably naive conclusion that while sexual stimulation may have been the precipitating factor in causing a man to make his first purchase, his collector's pride then came to the fore, and motivated him to continue to buy the material.

One major criticism of this Commission was that the commissioners had so little direct contact with actual pornography. If they had personally and individually been exposed to this type of material for a good long period of time, they may have discovered if it really satiated the appetite.

In one piece of research done just a few years ago two psychologists recall their reaction to exposure to large quantities of pornography, "It seems to us undeniable that the vast majority of 'obscene' books fulfill their first and primary function of stimulating most readers erotically. This, at least, has been the subjective experience of the authors during their survey of literally hundreds of 'obscene' books in several major languages. Fortunately, or unfortunately, depending on one's point of view, the aphrodisiacal effect of 'obscene' books seems to follow the law of diminishing returns after a certain saturation point is reached. However, even at the end of this study, which necessitated the authors' overexposure to 'obscenity' in large quantities, neither the male, nor the distaff member of the research team could report on having achieved 100 per cent immunity to this type of literature."

"As to the small sample of people whom the authors interviewed with regard to the effect of 'obscene' reading matter, testimony was almost unanimous that they had been sexually stimulated by their reading."[2]

The intriguing aspect of this judgment is that these researchers were liberal in their attitudes, completely opposed to any form of censorship, yet in all honesty they had to report the continued aphrodisiacal effect of pornography.

The satiation theory misses the true nature of human sexuality and is sadly deficient as an argument for turning loose a flood of pornography on our society.

The Catharsis Concept

One of the most commonly used arguments in bolstering the case for pornography majors on the fantasy aspect of human, and particularly masculine, sexuality. People's sexual appetites need some type of satisfaction and because of the human's capacity to engage in fantasy, the argument runs, if we give him all the pornography he wants he will be able to live in the world of sexual fantasy, thus draining off his sexual energy leaving him without the need for overt sexual experiences.

From this perspective, making erotic art and literature available may actually have a highly beneficial effect on our society and save our women, particularly, from the advances of individuals who would otherwise be a menace.

The same argument has been used on behalf of violence on

television. The claim is that most people have a residue of hostility within themselves but they don't express this hostility, they are manifested through hostile acts. Therefore if they watch violence on T.V. they can vicariously live out their hostility. So the viewer gets it out of his system—drains it off.

It is strange that people will continue to give credence to these catharsis theories particularly after the disillusioning experience of many psychotherapists who are having second thoughts about the whole concept.

For many years the so-called expressive therapies, based on the catharsis idea, seemed to almost monopolize the field of psychotherapy. The ingenuity of the psychotherapist has extended through the bubbling of free association, the encouragement of verbalization in client-centered therapy, the hypnotic trance in which conscious control was reduced, narcotherapy which used chemicals, play therapy, puppet therapy, and a whole raft of similar expressive therapies were called in to facilitate full emotional expression.

Despite all this work and the inventiveness of the practitioner of expressive therapies the results were frequently far from satisfactory and in some instances downright disappointing.

A psychotherapist attending a small conference of educators was amazed at the outbursts of a fellow conferee. He came to know the man as the conference progressed, and one day while alone together, the psychotherapist suggested that his newfound friend's statements in the meeting had been rather strong. The fiery-tempered one looked at him in amazement, "But I have always understood from you fellows that I must not bottle up my feelings and that I was following good practice by expressing my emotion." Many a psychotherapist pondering the outbursts of his counselees and noting their lack of progress, has had second thoughts about the adequacy of the "expressive therapies" in bringing about life-changing experiences.

There are many people, like the man at the conference who not only find their hostility is not drained off, but as they express it, they become aware of new areas of hostility and sometimes finish up more antagonistic and hostile than when they began. Some psychologists are now saying hostile acts lead to hostile feelings. As one behavior modifier puts it, "As go our actions so go our feelings." Hostile acting out becomes part of a vicious cycle that leaves the subject in a worse emotional state than when he started.

The Pro-pornography group who have a penchant for claiming they have scientific evidence for their point of view have conveniently ignored many of these aspects of psychological research.

One thought provoking sidelight to the whole catharsis argument comes with a news item from *Variety*, the trade publication of the entertainment world. Discussing some of the problems with skin-flick theaters of New York City the paper notes the exits of these theaters are the favored spots for prostitutes on the lookout for customers. Patrons of the skin-flicks having been sexually aroused by the presentations provide a ready made clientele for the street walkers.

Pornography seems to have had very little catharsis effect here.

The Denmark Argument

In any discussion of pornography and its effects the investigator must stand ready to hear the argument, "In Denmark they removed all prohibitions on pornography, and their society is much better for removing these restrictions on individual freedom."

The new permissive legislation in Denmark took effect in August, 1968, and July, 1969, and in April, 1970. *Playboy* magazine, always on the alert to discover what will justify their own stance, made a great point about the fact that the sales of pornography had dropped and best of all the rate of sexual crimes had declined rapidly.

With that attitude which characterized the propagandist *Playboy* had conveniently ignored a UPI report out of Copenhagen dated January 10, 1970. The item told of Danish criminologists cautioning observers against crediting the reduction of sex crimes to the new law. These authorities pointed out that the figures showing a 31 per cent drop in sex crimes were misleading when used as a before and after comparison. The "before" figures include public indecency, voyeurism, male prostitution, and the sale of pornographic material, but once the new laws were enacted these activities were no longer considered to be criminal acts. This meant that taking before and after numbers was comparing two dissimilar figures. Incidentally, the cases of rape and sexual assault had not changed in their rate of occurrence.

What obviously happened in Denmark was that the law changed, not the offenses. As one observer commented, "If burglary were made legal, the Copenhagen crime rate would fall still further."[3]

To this the Deputy Chief Constable of Police in Copenhagen added yet another consideration, "There is reason to believe that the figures are even less reliable, because the regular exposition of pornographic material and the general abuse heaped on any one who seeks to oppose it has lessened considerably the willingness of the ordinary person to complain even of those activities which are still illegal."[4]

Quite a revealing comment from a man whose work is in the area of crime in Copenhagen itself.

When a British research team investigated the crime statistics they discovered another interesting facet of the situation. Danish authorities provided them with some information which read, "The number of sex crimes registered by the police in each of the years from 1963 till 1969, according to official figures is as follows:

>   1963—4,364
>   1964—3,968
>   1965—4,316
>   1966—4,210
>   1967—3,275
>   1968—3,060
>   1969—2,819

The British group were quick to note that the number of sex crimes had dropped right through the sixties and "The biggest single drop appears to have been between 1966 and 1967, i.e. *before* the new laws came into force."[5]

We might also note that even though the sales of pornographic literature were said to have declined, it was estimated by the *Copenhagen Times* that the Danish pornographic market stood at about $35,000,000 with exports amounting to $65,000,000 which is not a very low figure for a country with a population of 4,800,000 people.

Another facet of this example almost completely ignored was the boom in visual as against printed pornography once the former became legal. For the users of pornography, visual material would obviously have much more appeal than printed and probably accounted for the decline in the printed material. Even so, the *Copenhagen Times* reported that some 50 porno shops were now clustered around Copenhagen's main rail station to welcome the visitor as he left his train to enter the promised land of sexual freedom.

Of course *Playboy* magazine wants to make the most of every situation. The news in 1970 that crime had dropped in Denmark had, as we noted, brought cheers from *Playboy* but the statistics of crime in America were dealt with in a different manner. In the portion of *Playboy* called News Forum where news items of particular interest to readers are reported, *Playboy* called attention to the 1972 American crime statistics in which the rape figures were higher than ever before.

The report stated that the first quarter figures of 1972 showed a 2% rise in the violent crime rate but forcible rape has risen an alarming 17% in the same period.

Naturally *Playboy* saw no connection between the soaring forcible rape cases and the increasingly liberal laws concerning pornography. It was simply they said, that women were now more ready to report such cases to the police, and cooperate with them in catching and convicting rapists.

So for the pornography propagandists there are always two ways of interpreting crime statistics.

In any case the whole argument of crime statistics may easily divert us from some of the most important effects of pornography. We just don't know all the outcomes although there is much evidence to show many crimes to be pornography related, and it may take a couple of generations before we see what will be the long range effect. Moreover the damage may be much too subtle to gauge with statistics as it affects people's finer susceptibilities, their relationships with each other, and above all the quality of family life.

Another practical little matter is indicated in some recent figures on the incidence of venereal disease. An article in *Newsweek* highlighted the rising tide of gonorrhea in the United States of America which now has an incidence of 300 per 100,000 population as compared to such western nations as Britain, 118 per 100,000 and France 30 per 100,000 but in Denmark the ratio is 319 per 100,000. Apparently the Danish public health aspect was not enhanced by the permissive attitude.

A tragic footnote to the Denmark situation is seen in a UPI release which states:

"They look like a row of demure school girls. School girls they are. Demure they are not.

"The 12 and 13-year-olds lining the bench are sitting in a state-run venereal disease clinic. And they have given Denmark a new worry."

One doctor made a pathetic comment, "I am not preaching morals, but some of the youngsters in these days get venereal diseases the way the older generation got a hang-over."

In any case, to follow madly on the heels of any country's experimentation may prove to be hazardous. In my adolescent days the prime example of permissive sexual attitudes were supposed to be the French. When ever the boys wanted to whisper stories of strange and unusual sex practices they would preface it with the phrase, "In France they . . . "

A survey made in France in 1972 entitled *Report on the Sexual Behavior of the French* showed some sort of a shift in French sexual habits. Although the widely painted picture was of a Frenchman with a mistress, 70 per cent of husbands polled for this report, and 90 per cent of wives, said they had never committed adultery and 50 per cent of these polled considered unfaithfulness as unforgivable. The report concluded that as far as France is concerned, " . . . the oft advanced theory of declining morality is not borne out."[6]

Let's give the Denmark situation some time to settle down before we begin quoting it as an example.

Shakespeare who so often comes up with an expression of the human dilemma has a significant word when he makes Marcellus say in Hamlet, "Something is rotten in the State of Denmark."

The Educational Pitch

Pornography's most advanced and fraudulent claim is that it is part of a great educational endeavor. The thrust of this argument is that most Americans are sexual illiterates. They have been kept in ignorance across the years by the Puritan ethic. Because of this ignorance it is necessary to launch a massive educational campaign to dispel the dark clouds of sexual ignorance that has long engulfed the American outlook.

A typical publication of this type calls itself *The Journal of*

Sexual Communication and bears a caption, "educational material—for adults only." In the text the author deplores the sexual ignorance of Americans and states, "Most intelligent Americans are eager to rid themselves of the remnants of paranoia and guilt which their Puritan ancestors bequeathed them."

Then comes the pious statement that sex education materials can be divided into two neat groups, "the scientific euphemized textbook and the vulgar slang-ridden sex book." This leads naturally to the angle that repeats itself monotonously in pornographic literature, "Most educational materials are either not illustrative at all, or illustrated so imperfectly that the learner hasn't the vaguest idea. of what the topic under consideration actually consists."

Because of these factors the publishers make a statement of purpose worthy of any professional journal, "It is for these reasons that the present volume has been dedicated in effect to bridging the gap between the faculties of the scientific and the barbarisms of the vulgar."

While the text is supposed to be educational, the pictures are, of course, by their own admission the main educational emphasis of the publication. The mismatch of text and pictures provides some ludicrous examples of the utter falseness of pornography. One part of the text undertakes to clear up a misconception about the technique of sexual intercourse known as "riding high" and quotes Masters and Johnson to the effect that the idea of "riding high" bringing a more satisfactory sexual reaction is based on a misconception.

Rather unfortunately for this point, the illustration which is the main contribution of this volume to the educational process, is of a man and woman having coitus and carries a caption to the effect that "riding high" improves sexual experiences. Thus the illustration perpetuates the fallacy which the text quotes Masters and Johnson as exposing.

The cover sells these publications, particularly when they are enclosed in cellophane packages so that the contents cannot be examined. One of these "educational publications" is called *U.S. News and World Views* with striking red, white, and blue cover and a stars and stripes motif. It rather gives the impression that the United States Information Agency or some similar government outfit is disseminating a special message about the American way of life to the whole wide world. What a let-down. The text is dreary pornography with pictures completely unrelated to the text. Instead of a feast of Uncle Sam's ideas we finish up with Danish pastry.

Yet another of these magazines calls itself *The Portable Marriage Counselor* and claims to be a compilation of "more than 200 questions about sex that you always wanted to ask . . . and their answers." Well, if these are the questions that tantalize the minds of men and women who are seriously interested in sex, they certainly have wandered off into some strange bypaths.

This particular volume, set out in encyclopedic fashion, to give it that educational appearance, lists a whole group of subjects under the letter "c" with the implication that it is just one of a series of volumes that will provide all one needs to know about sex.

The subjects, vividly illustrated and dealt with in this volume, are:

Cocoethes   uncontrollable passion
Catamism   keeping youths for unnatural sexual purposes
Coitophobia   an abnormal fear of sexual intercourse
Caprography   sexual excitement derived from writing vulgarisms about excreta
Copralaghia   receiving sexual pleasure from handling feces
Coprolalia   receiving erotic stimulation through use of offensive language
Coprophagy   sexual stimulation from eating human excrement
Coprophilia   addiction to filth or dung
Corybantia   sexual frenzy in which there is excessive movement of the body

Now just what educational purpose is there here? Many of the terms have been dug up from the back pages of an antiquated medical dictionary; the words chosen and the illustrative material that is used clearly show that while masquerading as educational, the publication is in actual fact nothing more than an effort to titillate the jaded voyeur by majoring on the most extreme sexual deviations.

If this is sex education wherever on earth are we headed?

One of the recommendations of the Presidential Commission's Report on Pornography stressed the importance of a viable program of sex education, and many a person completely in disagreement with most of the report would agree that sex education has been badly neglected in the past, and the ignorance of yesterday should be replaced with good factual information.

Yesterday's imprecise informal sex education had given our children the myth that babies came from cabbages, or were flown in by storks, or carried in doctors' black bags, but at least they had the virtue of being harmless and fitted into much the same category as the story of Santa Claus.

Now has come a new myth. Mary Miles Khan, editor of *The International Psychoanalytical Library,* commenting on an illustration in these so-called educational materials says, "if somebody did not know how intercourse took place, this picture would not tell them. It can only be there to help to sell the book."[7]

A recent count revealed there were at this time more than 1500 "manuals" published with the express purpose of helping people with their sexual problems. Many of these carefully specified they were for use by married couples. One can't help but wonder as to what effect studying some of these manuals will have on American marriages. Here might be a clue to the problem of our burgeoning divorce rate.

The "No Effect" Contention

The media serves many purposes, not the least important of which is entertainment. This entertainment takes many forms: "who-done-its," comedy, satire, drama, variety shows, and among these the explicit portrayal of sexuality.

From this perspective pornography is just part of the entertainment scene, and in much the same way as comedy presents life in its most ludicrous moments, so pornography presents a sometimes hilarious view of an important aspect of human experience. People will read or view it, chuckle over the content, then just shrug it off. Consequently, we shouldn't get all upset about pornography for it really doesn't hurt anybody.

To take this attitude means to reject the influence of literature or other types of media when all evidence indicates that they have a tremendous capacity to convey ideas and motivate people.

Politicians have certainly been fooled. The continuing crisis in the American political scene is the way the media is used in campaigning. Candidates engage high priced public relations agencies to plan the strategies for using the media in creating a good image of a candidate as someone who would make an admirable legislator and represent his constituency more capably than his opponent. This strategy worries a good proportion of the population who feel there should be some limitation on the amount of money a candidate can spend on using the media. But apparently the whole issue is academic—people's action patterns are not changed by what they see and read.

What ninnies these educators have turned out to be. For years they've been wasting their time and the taxpayer's money in pushing a philosophy, that when an individual is introduced to an idea it will have a tremendous power to actualize itself in changes on behavior. And all that money spent on books, projectors, libraries has just been frittered away on the foolish notion that ideas and concepts might change people.

Those stupid businessmen have really flubbed it. Although they are normally hard-headed and mighty cautious about what they do with their money apparently they've been pouring it all down a rat hole. In their misguided plans of action they have spent billions of dollars on advertising. Their ridiculous idea was to stimulate action. They want people to buy a deodorant, change the brand of tooth-paste they are using, eat a new type of bread that is more nutritious. Moreover they imagine they can actually create a demand for a product simply by telling people about it in glowing terms.

But they're all wrong—ideas don't influence behavior—so say the pornographers.

The big liberal assertion so frequently made is, "No girl has ever been seduced by a book." The statement, of course, is a gross oversimplification, and the Poet-Librarian, Felix Pollak, stated the situation very succinctly, " . . . the saying doesn't do the cause of literature any good, or the intellectual cause in general. If one denies the power of the word to do evil, one denies the power of the word to do good. In effect, one denies the power of the word. I prefer the healthy fear and awe of the written and spoken word, evidenced by censorious zealots, to the wishy-washy neutralism of the liberalist anti-censors."[8]

Just consider the influence of *Mein Kampf* in turning a nation into a dictatorship, or a Communist Manifesto in tearing down a society or the writings of Luther to spark the Reformation. All the great movements among mankind have had literature to inspire and bring forth programs of action.

This "no effect" argument should have "no effect" on our thinking.

The arguments used to bolster a "hands off" attitude towards pornography certainly make sorry reading and their perpetrators have produced very little evidence for their postion. They all have an artificiality about them, a certain contrived approach that makes them seem like enormous rationalizations for the operators of some money hungry people who care little for anyone's welfare but develop arguments to justify their actions.

Examination of the reasoning used in developing these contentions evokes memories of Dr. Johnson's famous analogy, "It is rather like a dog walking on its hind legs, it is not done well, and one wonders why it is done at all."

Chapter Ten

The Legal Muddle

The drab brown and yellow appearance of the sleazy building is a foretaste of the depressing interior of the porno book store. Books lining the walls have only one theme—sex—sex—sex of every imaginable variety and type, portrayed in explicable art and vivid tasteless prose. The display stands are cluttered with vibrators, dildos, sexual dolls, and the specials, packages of paperback books bound in cellophane that can be purchased like some grab bag, sight unseen—in one store they actually sell the stuff by the pound.

From this central area one doorway leads to a peep show section, where, by inserting a quarter, a brief tantalizing segment of movies of perverted sexuality can be seen, while a second portal gives access to a theater where the more affluent, for $4.00, can see a full-length pornographic film.

Presiding over this three-fold operation of book and appliance store, peep show and movie house, in an elevated position, like a monitor in a Charles Dickens orphanage, sits the clerk, keeping an eye on his clientelle—those being duped sometimes turn the tables—customers in this type of establishment have a bad reputation for shoplifting.

In the Federal Court of Dallas, Texas, a group of forty-five employees of the "adult" bookstore chain, of which this shop is a part, filed a suit against Dallas's top law officials seeking more than $70,000 damages. The suit incredibly claimed, that none of the defendants working in this pornographic menagery sells any books he knows to be obscene. The charge—Dallas law enforcement officials are trying to harass them out of business through numerous arrests.

It is typical of the legal muddle that we face today, that the

impudent marketers of pornography should, in a spirit of righteous indignation, be suing the allegedly repressive law enforcement officials.

If you wonder how this ludicrous situation has come to pass
you must spend at least some moments looking at the legal side
of the pornography problem. But be prepared for some brain
befuddling legal reasoning, for nowhere does the layman feel
more at sea, than when he tries to understand the reasonings of
legal minds as to what is meant by a seemingly simple word
like obscene.

There are five federal laws against the distribution of obscene materials in the United States. One of these prohibits the
mailing of obscene material, a second the importation of obscene materials into the United States, another interdicts
broadcasting obscenity, two laws forbid the interstate transportation of obscene materials or the use of common carriers
to transport such materials. The 1968 Anti-Pandering Act and a
1970 act authorize postal patrons to request no further mailings
of unsolicited advertisements.

In addition to these federal laws, forty-eight states have laws
prohibiting the distribution of obscene materials, and forty-one
states have statutes which contain some special types of prohibition on the distribution of sexual materials to minors.

When the non-legal reader sees this array of laws he immediately concludes that enforcing them should be a pretty straight
forward process, but he soon discovers this is not so.

The two big headaches which emerge are:

(1) How do these prohibitions square with the first and
fourteenth amendments to the Constitution that guarantee freedom of speech, which in legalism apparently includes printed
and other types of materials?

(2) What is meant by the word "obscene"?

The two questions, like some motif in a musical masterpiece,
are intertwined with each other in any discussion on the legal
aspects of pornography.

The final arbiter in matters of legal moment is the Supreme
Court of the United States, and to that august body many
people have looked in hope of some certain word to clarify the
obscenity situation. In early decisions of the Supreme Court it
had been assumed that obscene materials, like libel, profanity,
and blasphemy were not protected by the first amendment, and

there had been a consensus that the distribution of obscenity should be prohibited.

The landmark ruling came in 1957 and had to do with two men, Sam Roth, a publisher of erotica, and Daniel Alberts, the proprietor of a West Coast "mail order business in filth." Although in their appeals to the highest legal body in the land they pleaded the protection of the first amendment, the Supreme Court rejected this argument by a 7 to 2 majority.

In its decision the Court defined obscene materials to be those "which to the average person, applying contemporary community standards, the dominant theme of the material, taken as a whole, appeals to prurient interest."

Thus in the appeals, of what have been described as "two tawdry defendants," came the basic principle which was to be of the utmost importance in cases involving pornography in the courts of the United States.

In 1966, a case having to do with that old "classic" of pornography, *Fanny Hill*, gave rise to one of many no-clear-majority decisions of the court. The court reversed the obscenity finding by a vote of 6-3 but the majority of 6 was comprised of groups of justices who issued several separate opinions. Such no clear majority decisions are not binding on lower courts. Three justices, Warren, Brennan and Fortas, said in their opinion material could not be declared obscene unless it was, "Utterly without redeeming social value."

This single expression was destined to bring with it untold complications in the already difficult task of defining obscenity.

As courts struggled across the years to decide what was or was not pornographic the announcement of the formation of a Commission to look into the whole subject of obscenity and pornography brought a ray of hope. At the head of the tasks assigned to the Commission stood " . . . with the aid of constitutional law authorities, to analyze the laws pertaining to the control of obscenity and pornography and to evaluate and recommend definitions of obscenity and pornography."

Here at last, it was hoped, would be a certain word that would clarify the situation and prepare the way for some sharp clear-cut distinctions that would simplify the work of the courts.

Alas for the hopes of all who looked for guidance. The Commission itself was hopelessly split. The free speech, anti-censor, civil libertarian group was in the seat of power, but a vocal minority was willing to fight them all the way, and much of the conflict centered around the way in which obscenity was to be defined.

The members of the Commission not only failed to come up with a clear definition of obscenity for future reference, but they were at odds as to the precise nature of the existing situation.

The majority group wrote a clear statement into their report and in the section headed *Constitutional Limitations on the Definition of Obscenity* stated, "The prevailing view today in the Supreme Court . . . is that three criteria must all be met before the distribution of material may be generally prohibited for all persons including adults on the ground that it is obscene. These criteria are:

(1) The dominant theme of the material, taken as a whole, must appeal to a 'prurient' interest.

(2) The material must be 'patently offensive' because it affronts 'contemporary community standards' regarding the depiction of sexual matters.

(3) The material must lack 'redeeming social value.'

All three criteria must coalesce before material may be deemed 'obscene' for adults.

"Not so," responded the members of the minority group of Commissioners. They pointed out this was not a binding decision of the United States Supreme Court. The phrase, "utterly without redeeming social value," had not come from a majority of the Court, but was an opinion rendered by three Justices, Brennan, Warren, and Fortas, and a three out of nine Justice opinion was not really a Court decision.

The minority Commissioners concluded, "The Roth case has given us only the prurient interest test and this test has not been modified by any subsequent Supreme Court decision. In Roth the court said, an item is obscene when to the average person, applying contemporary community standards, the dominant theme of the material taken as a whole appeals to the prurient interest.[2]

The lines had been drawn, and the two groups of contenders gathered around these two definitions. Those opposing the indiscriminate distribution of pornography were clinging to the Roth definition while the no-control group majored on the "redeeming social value" idea, primarily because it had the effect of providing no definition at all.

In a courtroom in Manhattan in 1973 a judge deliberated a verdict on a movie called *Deep Throat* described as, " . . . the story of a rapacious girl named Linda Lovelace. In spite of dozens of greatly varied sexual experiments Linda is never really satisfied, never sees those well-known fireworks. It is only when she learns from a helpful doctor that her clitoris, for some strange reason, is misplaced and embedded in her throat that she is able to improve her sex life dramatically."[3]

During the trial a group of witnesses appeared in court on behalf of the defendant.

* A movie critic said the movie, " . . . shows sympathy for the idea that woman's sexual gratification is as important as a man's."

* A psychiatrist echoed the idea that women didn't have to be exploited by men, and the portrayal showed, "a young woman who seeks organismic pleasure for herself."

* A medical psychologist, " . . . it puts an egg beater in people's brains and enables them to think afresh about their attitudes and values."

The purpose of all this evidence in the case of a pornographic movie involving what one writer described as an "anatomical absurdity"—to show this debased pornographic movie had "redeeming social value."

The expression, "redeeming social value," turns out to be an enormous hypocrisy for it provides a convenient loophole by which marketeers of pornography can evade any legal restrictions on their activities.

Pornographers have not been slow to capitalize on the legal situation, and many of them employ special lawyers who spend their time defending clients from charges having to do with obscenity and pornography. An article in the *Wall Street Journal* told of an attorney out of Houston who was grossing in excess of $200,000 a year from his law practice. His specialty—travelling around the country defending pornographers.

The work of local law enforcement agencies is complicated by a number of circumstances:

*Many local prosecuters lack the expertise to handle obscenity cases, especially when they find themselves facing a highly specialized defense attorney.

*The judgments of higher courts have often been so confusing that the prosecutor faces the possibility that his case will be thrown out on a technicality.

*Many prosecutors are burdened with a multitude of other problems associated with law enforcement.

*Naturally, when compared with such matters as rape, assault, and burglary, pornography incidents are down the priority list.

*Defense attorneys try to delay the prosecution as long as they can, using every gimmick and tactic. They believe that with material becoming progressively more salacious theirs will appear innocuous at a later date.

*Another tactic is to get the case into federal courts which adds a whole new level of complex paper work and causes prosecutors to back off.

When they do get convictions law enforcement officials are often faced with a disappointing sequel. One report on the actions against pornographers in Dallas, Texas, lets us see some of the problems from a police perspective: "We do not have the authority to close private businesses, only to file charges against the owners and operators when violations of the law are observed . . . . During the past 12 months, 47 cases have been filed against persons for exhibiting obscene movies and 76 cases have been filed against persons for selling obscene material. Fourteen cases have been tried and in each case a guilty verdict was returned. Sentences have not been probated except in three cases. All guilty verdicts are now on appeal.

"The profits in pornography are so enormous that fines alone will have no effect in controlling obscenity. Pornography in Dallas will continue to grow until the panderers are caused to serve maximum jail sentences. The maximum penalty is six months in jail and $1,000 fine . . . "[4]

Getting Off the Mailing Lists

One of the few pieces of legislation geared to helping the local householder was a post office regulation which allows a person to request that his name be taken off the mailing list of a pornography publishing house. If the publishing house continues to mail the material the responsible person may be imprisoned for five years or fined $5000 or both.

Although this regulation is often quoted to indicate that a

person doesn't have to be worried by this sort of material being mailed to his home, in actual practice it doesn't work out so well.

One man tells his story, "Two advertisements were mailed to Salt Lake residents soliciting orders for pornographic films, books and magazines. These advertisements were sent unordered and unwanted. One comes from a Los Angeles firm and the other from a Danish firm (which apparently purchased a mailing list from an American publisher). Both advertisements show explicit depictions of fellatio, cunnilingus, heterosexual intercourse, homosexual relations, and one shows females engaged in intercourse with animals. Sending these advertisements into homes, unordered and unwanted, represents, in my opinion, a serious invasion of one's privacy. Yet there is no legal way these can be stopped. In the case of the advertisement mailed from Los Angeles a false and non-existent California return address is given, but the instructions require one to mail the money for wanted goods out of the country. Thus the Los Angeles firm uses an out-of-the-country mailing post, where they escape the penalties of our local laws, collect their money, then mail back through our post office service the illegal material."

Already over half a million people have gone to the trouble to fill out these rather difficult forms, but because of the subtlety of the pornographers, hopeful householders may have been wasting their time.

Victimless Crimes

Among the more sophisticated members of the community it has become increasingly fashionable, when discussing pornography, to launch into a discussion of victimless crimes. Having made an impression with a new phrase, the protagonist proceeds to point out that there are statutes on the books against crimes without victims—prostitution, gambling, vagrancy, and in some instances narcotics.

In a peculiar manner, many of these people, who have never had a second kind thought about law enforcement officers, become very concerned about the way these officers are so terribly overworked, and they argue that while the lawmen are giving their attention to victimless crimes they are missing an opportunity to do something about offenses that involve other people like burglary, murder, assault, etc.

While the idea may be attractive at first glance, more considered thought indicates that these are areas that need deeper evaluation.

Of course, victimless crimes is a contradiction in terms.

The drug addict who must have increasingly larger sums of money to support his habit and who is in need of a fix assaults and robs. No victim?

A gambler getting deeper in debt can't pay and finishes up in a pile of cement at the bottom of the river. No victim?

The pretty girl not doing so well falls into the hands of a pornographer who pushes her into modeling a whole series of perverted activities. No victim?

The prostitute whose customer may be mugged or robbed. Or the client who contracts a venereal disease which he spreads around the community. No victim?

Read in the following chapter the case against pornography and ask yourself if it is really victimless. No matter how it is expressed there are always two major victims, the family and the community, and many others whom it leaves strewn in its pathway.

The law often protects us against our own follies and although this statement brings a howl of dismay from people who conjure up visions of a fascist society in which storm troopers take over every aspect of our lives, in actual fact the law has a certain paternalistic aspect. Our government won't let us grow old without making some provision, so we are compelled to subscribe to social security. Contemporary Mormons, who have given us excellent examples of the way in which they care for their families, may have a yen for polygamy, but the law tells them they cannot live this way.

Even if no other person is involved, can we stand idly by and watch a man destroy himself? Kristol suggests an extreme case in which a playwright may be presenting a play that calls for suicide. He might be able to find some person who would be willing for a sum of money to commit suicide on that stage in front of the audience. Should we let him?

The pornography issue is always tied up with the well-being of society, and most societies are concerned about activities that affect their total life. Ancient Rome finally realized that gladiatorial exhibitions were hurting the populace. Bern makes a strong case that no society is unconcerned about the manner in which its citizens entertain themselves. So bear baiting and cock fighting are prohibited not only because of the suffering to animals but because of the way these sports brutalize the citizenry. Similarly with public hangings.

Pete Hamill states the situation very clearly when he calls for some level-headed thinking about the effects of pornography, then says, "If the stores were flooded with books advocating the physical violation of Jews, there would be an uproar. If those books were about castrating and torturing blacks, there would be court orders everywhere.

"If they were defenses of segregation or apartheid, we would be revolted. Instead, pornography is among us in a flood, designed to incite cruelty and violence against other human beings who do not fit into any 'acceptable' category. Just women. Just objects."[5]

American justice takes some strange turns. An overparked car can bring a peremptory fine or in the case of a speeding ticket the judge gives the impression that he would not dream of doubting the officer's word and summarily dispenses justice, but pornography can evade the law by using such terms as "social redeeming value," raise legal technicalities, and protest about victimless crimes.

The aesthetic factor demands consideration. We fine people for littering, and many an owner of a recreational vehicle has found himself living in a community where he cannot even park his trailer in the driveway of his own property. The city has an ordinance that says if he is going to keep such a vehicle he will have to park it out of sight in his backyard.

In New York, a few years ago, a strong-minded couple, wishing to show their displeasure with high city taxes, cluttered up the front yard of their house by erecting a number of clotheslines upon which they hung a jungle of disreputable clothing.

The city responded with an ordinance that required special permits for front yard clothes lines. The determined couple fought the city all the way to New York's highest court where the judge ruled against them and upheld the ordinance as one that, "based on what may be termed aesthetic considerations, proscribes conduct which offends sensibilities and tends to debase the community . . . "[6]

Washing on a clothesline!

Surely on the basis of anti-display statutes alone something should be done about the degrading displays seen at pornoshops and theaters compared to which washing on a line is a thing of beauty.

Organized Crime and Pornography

Nothing at the same time illustrates more vividly the fallacy of victimless crimes and the futility of a cloudy legal concept of the nature of obscenity than the way in which crime has linked itself up with pornography.

Many of the racketeers have moved in on the pornography scene, in part because they have discovered its enormous profits, but preeminently because they see the way in which confusing and contradictory legal decisions on obscenity have been handed down in courts. Ever on the alert for a legal loophole, they have seen that the distribution of pornography is much safer than gambling, selling heroin, and loan sharking.

An article in the *New York Times* has disclosed that organized crime families see pornography as their fastest growing racket. The activity is growing so rapidly that law enforcement officials claim it has surpassed all the rackets the "families" have developed in the last decade.

The racketeers have taken over the production and distribution of pornographic movies, books, and magazines, and are now extending their control to the burgeoning numbers of massage parlors that have sprung up in New York.

One attraction has been the large amounts of money that are involved. The *Times* reports that in 1968 "family" interests opened an operation on Staten Island to mass produce hard core pornographic films. When federal agents raided one of these operation's distribution centers, they found 50,000 reels of hard core pornographic films. Investigation showed that these cost about $3.00 each to process and were retailed at prices ranging from $25 to $65.

In true "family" fashion the racketeers have entered into every phase of the pornography operation. Having ordered large quantities of pornographic books, after delivery they frequently ignore their creditors. As one expert put it, "If you're not paying anything for a book and you are getting $1.00 for it, and if you have printed close to one half million of those things you are making somewhere about 500,000 times $1.00." Moreover, with inferences of violent reaction many printing companies have been reluctant to press their claims.

A second source of revenue for the racketeers is "knock-offs." These are illegal reproductions of published works.

But the major opportunity for the racketeers is control of the outlets—the bookstores. Rake-offs come all along the way. Leasing arrangements are complex and conceal the identity of the lessee, some pay as high as $2-3,000 per month for store-front locations. Clerks are hired at $125 a week but can augment their salaries by under-the-counter sales. One witness testified about a Times Square location where an energetic clerk could earn as much as $500 a day extra.

The racketeers have even developed a certain subtlety in their work. One recent report says their latest films are mixing a story in with the assortment of sex acts, and then displaying films in commerical theaters—the angle, once the pornographic film has a story legal conviction is difficult because the film has "social redeeming value."

Are the crimes of these mobsters victimless?

The legal side of the pornography question demands some action by interested citizens. It isn't enough to sit down and lament, "Why don't the police do something?" The police have quite a task on their hands.

The procedure followed by the city attorney's department in Dallas gives us a glimpse into the complexity of their procedures in making a case against a pornographic movie.

(1) The officer first went to view the movie and having viewed it, came back and made an affidavit as to the facts surrounding the movie itself. He described it in some detail. This affidavit was attached to a motion for the issuance of a search warrant in the Criminal District Court.

(2) The Court then issued an order to the operators and employees of the movie to come show cause why a search warrant should not be issued and at the same time ordered them to keep the movie intact—either at the movie itself or, if they desired, they could bring it in the Court.

(3) At the same time the Court ordered a Deputy Sheriff to go to the theater and to sit in the theater or around the theater to be sure that the movie did not disappear and was not destroyed or altered.

(4) The Court set an immediate hearing on the issue of whether or not a search warrant should be issued.

(5) Following the hearing on whether or not a search warrant should

be issued based upon the testimony and the affidavit of the officer himself and any persons that the defendants desired to bring in the Court, the Court then issued a search warrant.

(6) Following the issuance of the search warrant, the Sheriff went out and picked up the film from the movie projector and brought it back into Court and it will now be submitted to the Grand Jury for their action.

(7) The Court gives to the defendants an opportunity within three days' time, to come in and to ask for a complete hearing on the obscenity of the movie if they so desire—or anyone else who is claiming an interest in the movie may come in and ask for such a hearing.

The city attorney admits that in using this method, "It is cumbersome and takes man power," but sees it as the only viable way of doing the job. It doesn't take much imagination to see how discouraged the law enforcement officers can become. Such a complex process followed by difficult court procedures could easily lead law enforcement officials to believe they should expend their energies in more profitable fields.

In one area pornographers are willing to give a little. They are not altogether opposed to legislation that will make obscenity material illegal for juveniles. But before you marvel at their change of heart, think again. Material marked "Adults Only" floods the newsstands where it whets the appetites of juveniles. The newsstands do not police their sales, and the stuff finally finishes up in young people's hands. Pornographers are the preeminent Indian givers.

A Writer's Suggestion

"As a writer I am professionally interested in sex, since it provides the artist with a large portion of his best material. In my novels dealing with the great conflicts that engulf men and women in love, I have written about some fairly robust situations."

Any reader of celebrated author James Michener's books would agree with his own assessment of the way in which he uses "erotic realism" in his writings. But faced with the portrayal of sadistic, masochistic, cruel and perverted sex in writings that are getting into the hands of juveniles, this noted writer has issued a call for action against pornographers.

With the thoroughness that characterizes so much of his

work, Michener turned his attention to the legal situation. As a result of this research, Michener came up with a suggestion as to the way the legal system should handle the problem of pornography.

Michener makes the point that the Supreme Court has painted itself into a corner by ruling on cases involving individual books and movies and quotes the statement of Justice Hugo Black, "My belief is that this Court is about the most inappropriate supreme board of censors that could be found. So far as I know, judges possess no special expertise providing exceptional competency to set standards and to supervise the private morals of the nation. In addition, the Justices of this Court seem especially unsuited to make the kind of value judgments . . . as to what movies are good or bad for local communities."[7]

As a way out of this impasse Michener comes up with a three-fold program.

(1) The Supreme Court should refuse to review individual works to determine whether or not they are pornographic.

(2) Congress should pass a law empowering the highest courts of the fifty states, or subsidiary courts nominated by the states, to serve as courts of last appeal as to whether a work is pornographic.

(3) Each state would thus return to the principle enunciated in Roth of "applying contemporary community standards" in judging pornography. Trials would be by a jury of citizens, who would be presumed to know what the standards of their community were. If they ran hogwild and turned in arbitrary or illegal verdicts, a higher state court would redress the balance."

With almost prophetic insight—Michener wrote in 1968—the celebrated author quoted Judge Samuel Hofstadter, of New York's Supreme Court, "Essentially the problem of obscenity is one of municipal order. It is not intrinsically a constitutional question. Hence it cannot be decided properly at the summit but must be disposed of at the base."[8]

And now it seems as if there is a move to return the legal processes from the pinnacle to the base and make state and local laws of increasing significance in dealing with the problems of obscenity and pornography. At this level the local citizenry regain faith in our judicial system. After a period in which they have watched highly paid lawyers circumventing what seemed to be obvious laws, the common citizen begins to feel his faith in our system being renewed again. In his community, rather than far off Washington, or some other central spot, he sees the law at work to protest the weak and restrict the malevolent exploiters.

The time has come for the citizenry to stand up and demand a rigid enforcement of the law. For too long all the concern has been about the fear that the law might impinge upon the pornographer's freedom of expression. While we allowed him to practice his corrupt craft we overlooked the nature of pornography of which Lord Longford's report said, "Pornography represents an all persuasive assault on the freedom of the individual," and failed to concern ourselves with the pornographer's victim. We must turn the tables and let the law protect the weak and restrict the exploiter.

Chapter Eleven

The Indictment Against Pornography

What do Justice Potter Stewart of the Supreme Court and Senator Barry Goldwater of the U. S. Senate have in common?

They both know pornography.

Justice Potter Stewart, "I know it when I see it."

Senator Barry Goldwater, "As a father and a grandfather, I know, by golly, what is obscene and what isn't."

Although they are aware of these subjective reactions, these two men in the highest legislative and judicial bodies of the land have struggled with the problems of definition and control.

What chance then has Mrs. Nordan in discussing the matter with Jimmy? This widow, gravely concerned about her children's welfare, had found some really hard core pornography carefully stashed under her offspring's bed. After a long struggle within herself, she at last sat down to have a motherly talk with her son.

With ill-concealed impatience Jimmy turns on his mother, "What is wrong with girlie magazines?"

One of the tasks of this volume is to help the Mrs. Nordan's and others concerned with the question by summoning pornography before the court of factual knowledge and presenting an indictment—an indictment of eight counts.

1. **Pornography has created a mythical woman.**
2. **Family life is undermined by pornography.**
3. **Sex is divorced from love in pornographic presentations.**
4. **In its portrayals of sexuality pornography presents the wrong models.**
5. **The world of pornography is completely fictional and unreal.**

135

6. Pornography has misrepresented the true nature of human sexuality.

7. Pornography destroys the right of privacy.

Pornography Has Created a Mythical Woman

The major proportion of pornographic production is focused on the female of the species. She is examined in the minutest detail and theoretically by the time the reader gets through he should be an authority on the subject of womanhood.

Unfortunately for the would-be student of femininity the woman of pornography is a "woman who never was"—a myth.

The female portrayed in these pages exists only in the mind of the author or the artist.

She is a masculine wish-fulfillment. As the personification of feminine lust she spends her days tracking down males who will satisfy her sensuous desires.

Graphic evidence of this misrepresentation is demonstrated in the manner in which bestiality is portrayed in many of these writings. The predominant theme is the lust of the woman who is so concupiscent that she will stop at nothing.

But virtually no pictures of men involved in bestiality.

The real facts of bestiality are far otherwise.

Kinsey noted this in his research. His investigations had shown that boys growing up on farms were close to animal life and had apparently noted the similarity between animal and human anatomy and physiology. Moreover, in the discussion with other boys, and listening to adult men, sexual contacts with animals, actual or fictionalized, often became the subject for discussion.

The result of this, and other factors, was that seventeen per cent of farm boys, in the Kinsey survey, showed they had sexual contact with some form of animal life to the point of orgasm.

By way of contrast, only 1.2 per cent of Kinsey's female sample had ever been aroused erotically by an animal, and only a small proportion of these attempted actual coitus.

But Kinsey noted that in the archives of folklore and mythology there were frequent portrayals of females being involved with a wide variety of animal life.

Kinsey offered his explanation as to how this came about: "Much of this interest in rare or non-existent forms of sexual performance may represent the male's wishful thinking, a projection of his own desire to engage in a variety of sexual activities, or his erotic response to the idea that other persons, especially females, may be involved in such activities . . . Human males, and not the females themselves, are the ones who imagine that females are frequently involved in sexual contacts with animals of other species. In fact, human males may be responsible for initiating some of the animal contacts and especially the exhibitionistic contacts in which some females (particularly prostitutes) engage."[1]

Modern pornography has maintained the myth. If it were a realistic portrayal of sex that it claims to be, pornography would portray masculine bestiality instead of dealing almost exclusively with the fantasy of female bestiality.

Family Life Is Undermined by Pornography

Looking over all the damage done by pornography one casualty stands out preeminently—the family.

The message of pornography is anti-family. The emphasis on sex without relationship, its attack on the concept of a wholesome, well-rounded love, the downgrading of commitment to a mate that provides a setting within which children can be raised, all of these and a dozen other facets of the material cut away the very foundations upon which the structure of family life is built.

But the attack is even more insidious than it first appears, as it emerges as a massive propaganda campaign which, if carried to its logical consequences, will completely alienate young Americans from our traditional concepts of family life.

It has long been the custom of American male college students to screen stag films at surreptitious gatherings away from the watchful eyes of the school authorities. But no need of that anymore in many colleges. Pornography has quit going around to the tradesmen's entrance and has gone straight up the front steps of the main administration building. It is rapidly becoming so respectable that it may not be long before a puzzled parent will hear the news that Jeannie has signed up for an interesting course, Communication 3442, "The Use of the Media for Eroticism."

Two characters, of whom one is a former writer for the filthiest of all the underground newspapers and the other active in publishing ventures, have been cutting quite a swarth in the pornographic field. They started by running an Erotic Movie Festival in New York, and then teamed up with a lecture bureau, claimed to be "the world's largest lecture agency," with the objective of bringing pornography to the campus.

A newspaper reporting the project headlines it "Pornography Wises Up and Goes to College." The program consists of 45 minutes of erotic shots with ten minutes of comments by the two self-confessed experts in erotica.

The content of the presentations comes from a selection of the films submitted for the Erotic Film Festival and is heavy on elaborate camera shots. One of the presenters discussing a five minute examination of the human genitals says, "To really appreciate this, you should have a picture on a forty foot screen."

Coincidental with this development, courses are being offered on many college campuses today typically titled "Alternatives to Family Life." The editor of *The Journal of Marriage and the Family,* who reviews books on family and marriage and across whose desk most of the recent publications on the subject come, states, "Publishers are knocking themselves out to print books that predict marriage is finished and offer alternatives to marriage and the family."[3]

One of the most widely used volumes which is required reading in these types of courses on something like 150 campuses from Maine to California is *The Family in Search of a Future.* Some of the alternatives to family life suggested in this volume are group marriage, homosexual marriage, sex outside marriage, communal families and polygamy. One chapter in this book dealing with the subject of polygamy speaks of "a new era when it is taken for granted that both men and women want variety in their relationships. Individuals look with an almost condescending smile upon the earlier period in which the standard assumption was that one would love only one person at a time."[4]

Just put yourself in the shoes of an impressionable kid in his freshman year in college. Newly concious of his freedom from the strictures of his home and not objective enough yet to really appreciate his parents and their values, he is becoming vividly aware of a pulsating sexuality. At this critical moment he is surfeited by a flood of materials depicting all the variants of human sexuality. He makes a visit to the "select series" in the student union where they are screening the juicy morsels from the erotic film festival, and to his ears there come the stories of the antics of other students in co-ed dorms or those living off campus in pairs, communes, or other types of association.

Stories whip around the campus about these various activities, and they naturally surface in class discussions or conversations with faculty members. The professors, ever on the alert for news of "needs" of students and eagerly watching for some opportunities to introduce "innovative courses," discover their opportunity.

With the bewildering speed that characterizes many of the changes in curricula that take place on American college campuses, a new course is introduced. Students are enrolled in a study of alternatives to the traditional forms of family life.

The ping-pong effect continues. Students, inundated with cheap pornography, talk about experiments with alternatives to family life. Teachers respond with new courses about other possible ways of coming at the problem. Students return to their own circles to quote the professor as an authority on the subject and use his prestige as a means of introducing others to these new experiments.

Two professors at a large state university asked about a course on *Alternatives to Family Life* responded by ennunciating a real problem, "There is no solid research evidence yet to tell us how the 'Alternatives to Marriage' work or to what extent they've caught on." The professor admitted they had to rely heavily on fiction—books like *The Harrad Experiment!*

The Harrad Experiment is a book about a fictionalized college in which students were assigned to rooms they share with a person of the opposite sex, and in the course of the book they allegedly tell about their activities in a series of journal entries. Anyone who has taken time to read this volume knows the highly imaginative nature of the portrayal. It is as the good professor acknowledges—fiction.

Of course fiction has a part to play in the college curriculum—in the English department, where literary skills are being taught—but hardly in the sociology, psychology, or family life departments. In these social sciences we need hard facts, and many of them are available.

For example, in a two-hundred-year period, from 1680 to 1880, the new and growing country of America witnessed a series of socialistic experiments that aimed at setting up what Holloway calls "Heavens on Earth" in this new country. These pioneering efforts at communal living, at their height involved more than a hundred-thousand men, women, and children who lived in a hundred communities scattered across the United States.

There are excellent documented accounts of the checkered careers of these groups and their ultimate demise.

In my own research of modern day communes I found plenty of evidence of what was going on, how short-lived they are and the devastating aftermath of these alternatives to family life as they left damaged kids in their train. But this factual information is ignored and classes are studying fiction. Is this part of the strange new world where fact is fiction and fiction is fact? Does it matter that impressionable students are encouraged in completely unchartered new ways of life because, "The professor seemed to indicate it's okay."

Sigmund Freud is often credited with propagating a theory that gave rise to many of the ideas of freer sexual expression, but a closer examination of his writings shows that his main emphasis was upon the environment within which the child spent his early years of life and its relationship with its parents during this time period.

Historically the family has been a microcosm of a wider society within which the family members have learned relationship skills that will prepare them for the broader experiences of life. Fundamental to a good family unit is a husband and wife committed to each other, and providing not only an economic basis but a warm loving climate for the development of personality within which the children will see models of masculine and feminine roles and examples of man-woman relationship.

To present an adequate picture of family life demands the denial of the false fictions of pornography.

Sex Is Divorced from Love in Pornographic Presentations

Although the pornographer may use such expressions as "making love," "let me give you love," "love child," or "the act of love," love is one of the four-letter words about which the pornographer has virtually no knowledge and he is an expert in the use of four-letter words.

The implication of most of these writings is that the words "sex" and "love" are synonyms. However, there is a tremendous amount of evidence to show that this is not so.

* Sex is basically physical, stemming from body chemistry and capable of response to purely physical stimulation: on the other hand, even though love includes the physical, some of the greatest love affairs have involved very little physical contact.

* The sexual response mainly concerns only one aspect of conscious process—the emotional; love at its best consists not only in how the individual *feels*, but how he *thinks* and how he *acts*.

* Sex is fundamentally selfish and the sexually aroused person may seek satisfaction without consideration of anybody else; love is a concern for someone else and the lover will forego sexual experiences in the interest of his beloved's welfare.

* Both man and beast share sexual drives; love is a cultural development that has no counterpart in animal or insect life.

* Sex in its most urgent forms does not discriminate; love sees a partner with whom relationships grow and develop.

With these distinctions in mind we can see that in the development of mankind the wedding of the concepts of sex and love as a viable unitary human experience has been one of the greatest moves forward, and any effort to separate them might well be a step back to barbarism.

Writing in a magazine on human sexuality a recent author told the story of the Marquesan Islands. Although a factual report by an anthropologist and entitled "Love Marquesan Style," it turned out to be an account of the way in which love and sex can be divorced.

These islanders are said to be sex experts. Children are initiated into sexual practices in their early days and learn how to gain the greatest pleasure from sensual experiences.

The writer of the article claims that in the early days when the European whalers and traders came to the South Seas the stories of the sexual capacities of these natives, like those of the sirens of old, lured the crews of the ships to the Islands. They brought venereal disease with the aftermath of decimation of a goodly proportion of the population.

Twenty years after his original contact with the depopulated islands the author revisited the scene and discovered population boom as the ancient sex patterns were reintroduced and the writer notes with approval, "Sex is what brought their assassins to the islands—and now sex was going to give them a place in the sun."

After commending all this "freedom from inhibition and sexual hangups" the author notices one slight difficulty, "I have never found, in the many years that I have voyaged through the island of Polynesia, an instance where a native woman fell deeply in love with her lover. She doesn't seem to have the emotional depth, or capacity to become seriously involved in permanent attachments with her lover."[5]

Is this good?

The sociopath or psychopathic personality presents the psychotherapist with a stubborn challenge. One of his major problems is that he cannot develop any depth of relationship with people and sees them only as objects for exploitation.

This is a primitive society, and one of the reasons it is primitive is that men and women have never learned about the bonds of fidelity which provide the basis for the development of family life.

One of the tragedies of our age is our mobile rootless society. What people need more than anything else—even sex—is a sense of a secure relationship.

A writer in a "soft core" porno magazine for women seeks to teach his female readers the delights of sensuality. In an unaccustomed note of candor he tells them, "Detaching love from sex may be the first step," and urges these gals to, ". . . enjoy the prospect of sex independent of the deep relationship demanded by love."

A cartoon in a typical porno-publication shows a girl and man stretched out on the floor of the apartment. He has called to take her out on a date and apparently they went into a sexual embrace. The girl is saying, "You mean that's it. That's our date?"

This is pornography's message—sex without love—without relationship—just sex that's all.

In Its Portrayals of Sexuality Pornography Presents the Wrong Models

When exhibitors tried to import the movie *Skyjack* in Australia the custom and excise Minister Donald Chip refused permission and explained his action by saying, "The film deals with the hijacking of a crowded civil airlines by a mentally disturbed U. S. Army Sergeant. The method of hijacking and of holding a crew and passengers hostage are explicitly and vividly depicted . . . The experiences of airlines and civil aviation authorities have shown that the hijacking techniques employed in films are reproduced in real life a short time later."[6]

By his action Chip was showing that he believed in *imitative learning,* one of the hottest ideas in the field of education today.

Edgar Guest once said, "I can soon learn if you'll show me how it's done" and the older concept of apprentices working with experienced competent mechanics, carpenters, or masons was built on the idea that the apprentice watched the master craftsman at work and learned by imitating him.

Some of the new breed of psychologists called the "behavior shapers" have been particularly enthusiastic about these new-old techniques of learning by observing someone else and following his example and have used terms like modeling, vicarious learning, observational learning, identification to describe the process.

Even in the practice of psychotherapy the technique is being used. O. Hobart Mowrer, the brilliant learning theorist, advocates the use of, "modeling the role" by which the therapist trying to help his client "become open," opens up his own life by admitting his failures and shortcomings. The client generally responds by a similar response of openness.

Although Masters and Johnson used some esoteric techniques in their research with human sexual functioning when it comes to sex education they advocate a method that is the essence of simplicity. Masters describes the teaching procedure which he suggests, "There is nothing that teaches sex half so much as Pop patting Mom's fanny as he walks by her in the kitchen. Obviously she loves it, and the kids watch and say 'Boy that's for me.' "

But what if instead of seeing Daddy make an affectionate gesture towards Mother, he sees brutality, force, sex without love, and the callous exploitation of women, won't he identify with these?

If we admit the influence of models in an individual's life, pornography spells menace to any person learning to function as a sexual being.[7]

A thirteen-year-old boy attacked a girl in an office. He later related that the idea had come to him from an article he had read in a stag magazine replete with a portfolio of nude pictures of women and containing an article, "How to Strip a Woman."

This type of report occurs frequently. Police files are bulging with records that tell the monotonous story—a sexual offense—arrest of a suspect—discovery of a cache of pornographic literature over which the subject has been brooding.

A sexual offender told of his reaction to his collection of pornography, "You want to practice what you have been reading." Another, telling of his experience with erotic movies, "I would go to one, then go out and attack some woman." A convicted rapist said that from his reading of pornographic literature he was convinced women were eager for sex but when he approached them they rebuffed him and so he raped in retaliation.

One investigator after doing intensive research with sexual offenders incarcerated in two penitentiaries reviewed the evidence and concluded, "I remain deeply impressed that so many offenders in the two institutions implicated pornography as an influence towards crime."

The World of Pornography Is completely Fictional and Unreal

Seeking to find an analogous literary form, some workers in the field have suggested that pornography is sexual science fiction. While it is easy to see the similarities as to this form of writing, there are a number of notable differences. Probably the most important of these is that few readers of science fiction would ever try to build a rocket to travel to the moon or construct a micrononic ray to freeze people into plastic because they realize it is fiction and beyond their capacity or ability.

But in pornography the subject matter presents an experience apparently not only within the capacity, but as highly desirable, and the undeniable right of the reader.

If pornography is designated as sexual science fiction, we will note that it is decidedly weak on science and long on fiction, so strong indeed that it has little resemblance to factual sexuality.

It is true that it isn't always easy to draw a line between pornography and what has been called "erotic realism" in the media. However, we can make one clear distinction between pornography and other forms of discussion of human sexuality. In legitimate types the presentation takes place in context against the background of the wider influences of life.

Shakespeare and the Bible both deal with problems of sex and violence. Shakespeare in his plays presents some 52 violent deaths on stage and 64 behind the scenes. These experiences are subordinated to the plot of the plays and fit realistically into the ongoing portrayal. Similarly with the Bible. It speaks very frankly about sexual encounters, but it does so in terms of the events that lead up to the encounter, and then majors on the outcomes.

Pornography, on the other hand, presents sex out of context. As Van den Haag put it, "Pornography severs sex from its human context. It reduces the world to orifices and organs; incessant copulation without apprehension, relationship or love. It's the bare sensation of pain and pleasure. This reduction of life to varieties of sex is but the spinning out of unreal fantasies which upset the burden of reality and individuality, of conflict and commitment, thought and consideration. People are literally devoured, tortured, mutilated and dehumanized."

This may be the worst single aspect of pornography. We've spent time trying to speculate about the number of sex crimes that are the outcome of exposure to these materials, but the greatest casualties may be those from suggestible souls who gullibly swallowed the message and then were left with a sex hangup that may be with them for all their days.

The Pornographers Are Guilty of a Monstrous Hypocrisy

The writers of pornography who rail at hypocrisy with such an unctuous note, whine about the terrible damage of the Puritan ethic, and endeavor to show the double talk of religionists, are themselves guilty of the most blatant hypocrisy.

A beautiful example of this hypocrisy is the use of the terms "adult" and "mature" to describe X-rated movies.[8]

Use of the word "mature" to describe these meat market performances sounds might funny to a psychologist. One good definition of maturity is, "The capacity to postpone pleasure." Pornographic movies preach the gospel of immediate self-gratification, and in this and other aspects of personality are the complete negation of maturity.

Another "put on" with pornography are those books written by women in which they describe and extol in great detail masculine genital and copulatory capacity and the intense insatiable desire that seized hold of this particular woman's body. Kinsey reported, "Among the hundreds and probably thousands of unpublished, amateur documents which we have seen during the past fifteen years, we have been able to find only three manuscripts written by females which contain erotic elements of the sort ordinarily found in documents written by males. Similarly, out of the thousands of erotic drawings which we have seen, some of them by artists of note and some of them by lesser artists and amateurs, we have been able to find less than a half dozen series done by females."[9]

The same hypocritical note is seen in the books and films that are touted as "educational." At one stage someone hit upon the idea of a documentary film. Naturally the subject was Denmark, and inevitably this led to a discussion of sexual practices among the Danes with explicit portrayals of all this activity. The educational guise was also used in the era of the vogue for marriage guidance. Under the pretext of helping married people with their sexual adjustments every imaginable type of sexual functioning was portrayed.

It's the same old pornography wearing an academic gown and hoping to reach a new group with its wares.

Possibly the most hypocritical attitude of all is seen in the abuse of constitutional rights. Owners of theaters specializing

in X-rated films have bound themselves together in a "First Amendment" association. The operators of these sleazy out-fits, whose only aim is to gain a fast buck, proclaim they are fulfilling a patriotic obligation by running their shows, and any-body who objects is positively un-American.

With all its mealy-mouthed phrases, its deceptive practices, its prostitution of the words "education" and "patriotism," pornography is basically a monstrous hypocrisy.

Pornography Has Misrepresented the True Nature of Human Sexuality

Pornographers are the Barnum and Baileys of sexuality, and present The Greatest Show on Earth with a ballyhoo worthy of the most enterprising showman. The three rings of aerial artists on the high wire, equestrian acts, jugglers, animals leaping through flaming loops have their pornographic equivalent with the emphasis on action—slick, fast, and varied. One producer

of the genre of films called sexploitation says his formula is "one torrid sex scene every seven minutes."

Like Barnum, who believed there was one born every minute, the circus of sexuality presents the theme that performance is the thing—the most protracted and drawn out—the intense explosive climatic—the record breaking number—the contortionist positions—the elaborate paraphernalia—the dead heat conclusion.

The facts of human sexuality are far otherwise. Masters and Johnson, in their treatment of sexual difficulties, say this whole performance idea is erroneous. They warn against people "assuming a spectator role" in their sexual encounters. One commentator on their work adds, "Making efforts to coordinate such basically involuntary response, starts the partners observing themselves mentally rather than losing themselves in the act of love-making."

Like any good circus the pornographers have their freaks offering monstrous portrayals of aberrant sexuality. For those who enjoy gazing at animals with five legs, 400 pound women, dogs with two heads, pornography offers a field day.

A report out of Chicago tells about a police raid on a photographic studio. The officer in charge of the raiding unit said afterwards that the studio looked like a "medieval torture chamber."

In addition to 3,000 photographs, the police were fascinated by the props. These items included an old English rack, a chopping block, a sixteenth century stock, and assorted whips, chains, and handcuffs. Hooks were fastened to the ceiling, and some of the confiscated photographs showed models hanging from these hooks while being whipped. Some of the models were eleven and twelve-year-old girls.

For more ordinary people, looking at some of this pornography is rather like visiting the funeral home to view the corpse carefully dressed, coiffured, and rouged and having the undertaker murmur in one's ear, "Doesn't she look natural."

Pornography Destroys the Individual's Right to Privacy

Pornography is a massive attack on our personal, individual privacy. As Dr. Rollo May puts it, "The more powerful need is not for sex per se but for relationship, intimacy, acceptance and affirmation."

Once the pornographic movement really got under way it set about to examine every aspect of sexuality. An offshoot is the sort of radio programs which frequently run for as long as three hours each day. These programs go under such names as "Girl Talk," "Feminine Forum," and the announcer invites women to call in and discuss their problems. The callers give their first name, age, and city of residence and then proceed to discuss such topics as "Have you ever been unfaithful to your man?" Some exhibitionist females discussing their experiences, real or imagined, become so intimate they cannot be aired. But even this is grist for the announcer's mill. He makes the most of the situation. If it becomes necessary to blank out part of the dialogue, he comments on the activities being recounted with squeals of delight, "You did!" "Wowee" and gives the listeners imaginative hints as to what the caller is saying.

One of the most thoughtful evaluations of pornography has come from the pen of Irving Kristol who gives a moving example of the right of privacy. "Imagine a man—a well-known man, much in the public eye—in a hospital ward, dying an agonizing death. He is not in control of his bodily functions, so that his bladder and his bowels empty themselves of their own accord. His consciousness is overwhelmed and extinguished by pain, so that he cannot communicate with us, nor we with him. Now, it would be, technically, the easiest thing in the world to put a television camera in his hospital room and let the whole world witness this spectacle. We don't do it—at least we don't do it as yet—because we regard this as *an obscene* invasion of privacy. And what would make the spectacle obscene is that we would be witnessing the extinguishing of humanity in a human animal.

"Incidentally, in the past our humanitarian crusaders against capital punishment understood this point very well. The abolitionist literature goes into great physical detail about what happens to a man when he is hanged or electrocuted or gassed. And their argument was—and is—that what happens is shock

ingly obscene, and that no civilized society should be responsible for perpetrating such obscenities, particularly since in the
nature of the case there must be spectators to ascertain that
this horror was indeed being perpetrated in fulfillment of the
law.''

Kristol goes on to make the point, ''When sex is public, the
viewer does not see—cannot see—the sentiments and the
ideals. He can only see the animal coupling . . . When sex is a

public spectacle, a human relationship has been debased into a mere animal connection."[10]

That venerable champion of individual freedom Justice William O. Douglas, in voiding a Connecticut law against the use of contraceptives referred to the "zone of privacy" that surrounds the sex act. He stated that sex relationships involved a right of privacy older than the Bill of Rights. Pornographers please note.

The loud-mouthed protagonists of personal freedom should spend some time considering the right of privacy cherished by many people. The no-knock encroachment on the most personal aspect of human experience leaves many self-respecting individuals with the feeling that there is nowhere to hide. Everyone has a right to have a lock on his bedroom.

Katherine Anne Porter made a sensitive statement of the same principle, "Love-making surely must be, for human beings at our present state of development, one of the more private enterprises. Who would want a witness to that entire self-abandonment and helplessness? So it is best in such a case for the intruder to tip-toe away quietly, and say nothing. I hold that this is not prudery nor hypocrisy; I still believe in the validity of simple respect and regard for the dark secret things of life—that they should be inviolable, and guarded by the two who take part, and that no other presence should be invited."[11]

In trying to evaluate the mental condition of an individual, one of the most important criterion is—has the person good reality contact?

Looking at it from this perspective, pornography with its mytical woman, separation of sex from concern or involvement, its aberrant models, its fictionalized sex, its blatant exhibitionism is at its best madness, at its worst criminal.

Chapter Twelve

The Action Answer

Would the majority of Americans like to receive obscenity and hard core pornography through the mails?

Certainly not!

In a poll, 88 per cent of women and 80 per cent of men when asked this question answered with a resounding, "No."

This means then that if they were to receive such materials they would immediately take action—do something about it.

Right?

Wrong.

In the same poll the respondents were asked if they had ever personally taken any action to stop the sale of objectionable literature, and 94 per cent of the men and 91 per cent of the women answered in the negative.

These findings exactly spell out the problem we face today. The majority of Americans deplore what is happening; they feel it is wrong, something should be done to stem the tide. But they are calling for action from someone else, the police, the courts, the clergy, concerned citizens, but they cannot disturb themselves to take some personal action about the problem.

If pressed as to why they had not done anything many would probably respond, "I just mind my own business."

Clara Barton, the remarkable woman who started free schools, opened doors for women, and founded the American Red Cross, wouldn't have agreed with this attitude—her philosophy, "What's nobody's business is my business."

Pornography must be everybody's business. If we are going to make it our business we need to be aware of specific actions that should be taken.

The wife of a prominent surgeon attended a meeting of parents interested in the problems of drug abuse. After hearing a number of speeches about the enormity of the problem, one particularly eloquent speaker urged the parents to face the problem and "get involved."

The surgeon's wife, although she already had many social and civic commitments, volunteered her services with, "I want to get involved, what will I do?"

She later recounted, "What a let down! Apart from telling me to be a good mother and provide my children with love they had no plan of specific actions to really combat the menace."

The pornography problem is of major proportions, and looking at the size of it a concerned citizen can easily ask, "How can I get involved?"

Well, here is the answer. This proposed plan of action to stem the tide of mind-polluting obscenity, smut, and filth calls for the following actions:

(1) Make your voice heard.
(2) Present a positive view of sex.
(3) Mobilize public opinion.
(4) Hit them in the cash register.
(5) Enlist the women.
(6) Emphasize the consumer angle.
(7) Utilize the legal channels.

Make Your Voice Heard

It used to be that the mention of Denmark and Danes brought with it the image of high quality butter, ham, and other dairy products. Today the name Denmark and the expression "a Danish solution" conjures up visions of sex and society.

What is the most important lesson for us that comes from the Danish experiment?

It is *not* that a flood of pornography reduces sex crimes. We have seen the fallacy of that idea, preeminently it is that there are people in any society who, for the opportunity of making money, will subvert the will of the majority, and the Danish experiment demonstrates the old statement that all that is necessary for the triumph of evil is for good men to do nothing.

A lawyer from the Danish Department of Justice was being

interviewed by a journalist representing a pornographic magazine, and in the process the writer quizzed him about the dras-
tic change that took place in Denmark in 1966 when all laws
against pornography were summarily abolished.

The journalist asked, "Were there no vocal opponents to this
move?"

The lawyer responded that the state church had little social
influence and a spirit of lethargy had descended upon the nation and thus made it possible for a parliament which was
really dominated by conservatives to lift all its restrictions on
pornography. Then came the clincher as the lawyer said. " . . .
legislation would have been turned down if it had been put to a
nationwide popular vote."[1]

Confirmation of this situation came from the Deputy Chief
Constable of Copenhagen who in an interview said " . . . there
had been no general demand for the freeing of pornography.
The demand had been largely created and stimulated by newspapers and pressure groups."[2]

The United States of America came into existence on the
basis of a complaint. That complaint got action. People who
live in this republic must not hesitate to voice their grievances.
All too often we are sitting silent while we should be up and
speaking.

Within a democratic society every individual's voice and
vote count. And in the constant battle with pornography members of a free society must continually declare themselves. Experience has shown that the movie rating system will be
adjusted permissively as far as it can before there is a public
outcry, television shows and movies will be as permissive as
the public will permit them to be, and even the judicial system
itself despite its theoretical objectivity is aware of the way in
which the community is reacting in any given situation.

A Tennessee dentist demonstrated the power of a complaint.

Shades of the dirty speech movement. Morris Frank was
standing there reading from a pornographic book—a salacious
story laced with four-letter words—in public—in fact, in a
church building.

This practicing dentist, whom most people thought of as a
pillar of the community, thoroughly outraged the men meeting
in First Baptist Church for their monthly supper.

The men were not about to allow this sort of stuff. A deacon of the church was on his feet insisting that Frank had no right to read such smut in the church building.

The dentist had a quick comeback, "If it's bad to read it here, isn't it just as bad for your boy to read it, or for a boy to read it before coming to get your daughter for a date?"

The group of men got the message. Some reacted so violently that they wanted to prosecute anyone in town selling such literature, others suggested letters to the press, but the dentist finally persuaded them to make an approach to the City Council.

Frank had done his homework. He had noted some of the kids purchasing suspicious looking, soft-cover books and magazines, and dropped by the newsstand to look it over.

He was shocked by what he saw and later commented. "Some of these publications made *Playboy* look like a Sunday school quarterly. I realized I must act."

His resolution was strengthened when he read the sign on the wall, "No one under 21 permitted to read these novels," but noted teenage boys buying the material.

He started by talking with the owners and managers of the shops in question. Most of them gave him a good hearing, some promised action, but within a few weeks the situation was the same as ever, so he decided to enlist the men from the church.

Fortified now with the support of the men from First Baptist Church, the dentist checked over the state laws on obscenity and then appeared before the City Council. He followed the same procedure by reading from some of his samples of the pornographic books he'd bought in the shops and passed others around for the Council members to read. Then he posed the question, "Is this what you want your sons and daughters reading?"

The dentist so impressed the Council by the case he presented that they voted to enforce the state's laws.

On the following day the mayor and chief of police called on each of the proprietors or managers of the business concerned and they all agreed to cooperate.

Frank commented, "By nightfall the stores looked like The Religious Bookstore."

Mrs. Montgomery showed what a determined housewife can do. As she approached the checkout stand with a basketful of groceries she saw her son Tim, aged 7, walk over to the magazine rack, pull down a publication, squat on the floor and begin to read it so intently that she couldn't get his attention.

When she left her cart and hurried over to the boy, she was horrified by the porno magazine he had plucked off the bottom shelf to read.

Filled with indignation, Mrs. Montgomery approached the supermarket manager, pushed the publication into his hand, and announced, "If that's what you are going to sell on your magazine racks, I don't need to buy my groceries here and you can keep those that are in the cart."

The irate mother had helped the manager reconsider the type of literature he should have on his shelves.

And you'll have to keep on speaking up. Don't for one moment imagine that one tremendous effort will do it.

Dr. Frank discovered this. His original action against pornography took place in 1967. As time went on he discovered the material would gradually reappear in shops and it was necessary to periodically look over the shelves and take action. Interviewed in 1973, he reported that five years of experience had taught him that every community needs a few watchdogs to keep an eye on the situation.

Individual actions you can take:

* Look over the racks at the markets and newsstands and see what type of material is being sold. If you see something to which you object, go tell the manager in a friendly way assuming he will cooperate.

* If you can't get cooperation try some direct action like Mrs. Montgomery. Sometimes groups of housewives fill carts with groceries, wheel them up to the checkout counter, then leave them as a protest.

* Take up your pen and write, write, write, write. Send in your letter to the editor of the paper to complain about X-rated movies or other displays of obscenity in your community.

* Keep your eye on television, and the moment you see a program that is off-color write to:
  1. The manager of the local station.
  2. The company that is sponsoring the program.
  3. The network.

* One effective way of doing this is to take paper and
envelopes to your Sunday school class, P.T.A.,
Women's Club, or similar organization and write letters
on the spot while you have the inspiration of the group.
Here is a sample of a letter you can provide:

Gentlemen:

I am writing in connection with the program [name of pro-
gram] *aired at* [time] *on* [date] *over station* [name of station].
*The program was offensive to me and my family, particularly
the language being used and the sexual scenes portrayed.*

*I regret that a network like yours which has given us such
excellent programming in the past should present this type of
material and hope that this will not be the future policy of this
station.*

Sincerely yours,

Here are the network addresses:

NBC
RCA Building
30 Rockefeller Plaza
New York, New York 10020

CBS
524 West 57th Street
New York, New York 10019

ABC
1330 Avenue of the Americas
New York, New York 10019

Public Broadcasting Service
1345 Avenue of the Americas
New York, New York 10019

Mrs. Johnson once told how an action changed a situation.
Her husband was campaigning for the Texas Senate seat in
1948. On the evening before the election Mrs. Johnson and a
group of her friends decided to sit down with the telephone
directory and begin calling people and soliciting their votes.
When the results of the election finally appeared, Mr. Johnson
had won the Senate seat by a mere 87 votes. This victory
ultimately led President Johnson to the White House.

Your voice might make all the difference in an important
issue—make it heard.

Present A Positive View of Sex

Many actions must be taken against pornography and unfortunately some of these have negative connotations, protesting, letter writing, complaining, organizing people for registering dissident opinions. However, there are some other actions that are distinctively positive, and preeminent among these stands a program of sex education.

Among all the other misrepresentations of pornography towers the fact that it is a program of sex miseducation. As a part of this topsy-turvy portrayal of human sexuality is a ranting against religion and the oft repeated claim that the Bible is anti-sex.

Nothing could be further from the truth.

The Bible is pro-sex!!!

An examination of the scriptures shows that their teachings are remarkably relevant to the situation we face today and there are five major themes in the biblical concept of sex.

(1) *Sex is creative.* Those who say the Bible is anti-sexual show their ignorance and have been listening to people's opinions rather than reading the Bible itself.

God said to our first parents, "Be fruitful and multiply," so men and women are exercising their sexuality at the command of God. We are the extension of God's creative activity.

(2) *Sex is for union.* The sexual element makes humans realize their incompleteness. God said, "It is not good for man to be alone." My sexuality constantly reminds me that I need my wife. And pleasurable sex is highlighted. Take a look at the Song of Solomon in Dr. Moffatt's translation. The bridegroom says:

> You stand there straight as a palm,
>> with breasts like clusters of fruit;
> me thinks I will climb that palm,
>> taking hold of the boughs!
> Oh may your breasts be clusters of fruit,
>> and your breath sweet as an apple! (7:7-8)
> (7:7-8)

> And the bride responds:

> I am my darling's, and he—
>> he is longing for me.
> Come away to the fields, O my darling,

let us sleep in the blossoms of henna,
and hie us at dawn to the vineyards,
to see if the vines are a-budding,
if their blossoms are open,
if pomegranates bloom;
and there I will give you caresses of love. (7:10-12)

The sexual element is the great unifying factor in a husband-wife relationship.

(3) *Sex is not to be exploited.* Although the Bible portrays the creative and unifying aspects of human sexuality, it also realizes that an individual's sexuality may provide one of his most vulnerable points.

In the Ten Commandments, of the six which have to do with man's relationship with man, three or half of them have something to say about regulating sexuality. The key commandment is, "Thou shalt not commit adultery." The Bible sees the monogamous committed relationship as providing the basis for a viable family life.

The thought life, so much a part of the pornographic scene, has been anticipated. The Tenth Commandment is, "Thou shalt not covet thy neighbor's wife," and Jesus warned against the lustful look which only thought of another person as a body to be conveniently used rather than a total personality.

(4) *No perversions.* Look over the range of perversions, and you will discover the Bible has something to say about homosexuality, sodomy, bestiality, incest, and warns against them.

Perversions frustrate the purposes of sexuality in creativity, union, strengthening family life, and the command of God is that they should have no part in the Christian's life.

(5) *Sex is to serve humans not to master them.* As important as sex is in the biblical portrayal, it is never viewed as the all-important force in life. The biblical portrayal of sex leaves no room for the view that if an individual does not give expression to the libido forces in his personality some sort of psychic damage may follow.

The Bible maintains there is another way. It anticipates the exercise of self-control and redirection of sexual energy. So Jesus said there were people who "made themselves eunuchs for the kingdom of heaven's sake" (Matt. 19:12).

The concept has been noted by some psychologists who refer to this phenomenon by using the word "sublimation."

In the peculiar world created by pornography the activity of swinging or wife-swapping illustrates the pornographer's view of human personality.

Some introductory rites have been devised to enable the couples to get into action with each other. Sometimes the original contact is made by phone, and the two couples agree to meet in one of the respective couple's homes. When they meet in the prearranged spot the process of evaluation gets under way.

As they look over their prospective partners, husbands and wives have developed a series of non-verbal cues by which each one can convey a message to the spouse. Sometimes the woman puts her hand to her ear to indicate her prospect looks good, and the husband may scratch his head to indicate that he wants to get something going with the other woman. Another series of signals indicates if they feel they are inferior and it is time to break off and get out of the house.

A friend of mine knowledgeable in the ways of auctioneering tells me this is the way they buy cattle at the state fair! ! !

What a contrast this is to the biblical view of sexuality and respect for people's personalities.

Mobilize Public Opinion

Go to the local theater and watch the sex-saturated movies, walk into the newsstand and see the dozens of porno magazines, turn on your car radio and listen to a sex talk show interrupted with songs with suggestive lyrics, and flee at last into your home to turn on your TV to be confronted by an off-color show.

An ordinary everyday citizen is likely to get the feeling there is nowhere else to go, we are completely surrounded—if this sort of stuff offends you, you must be one of a handful of peculiar people within the population that *doesn't* really *dig* the porno world.

Don't you believe it!

Most decent people share your views. Don't be intimated. Link up with like-minded individuals and make a concerted effort.

The publishers of indecent literature are very conscious of the potentialities of group pressures and are organizing their own groups. One soft core publication suggests, "Organize a group of like-minded people to combat the influences of the pro censorship organizations . . ."[3]

Prepare yourself for your task. If you're going to convince others you must be convinced yourself. Read the early chapters of this book carefully and face the evil of pornography. As Nigel Nicholson says of pornography, "It debases society, removes the distinction between right and wrong, reduces sex to the lowest common factor and elevates lust above love. . . . like untreated sewage its removal is an act of social hygiene."[4]

Get together with a few like-minded people and make your plans. The pastor of your church might be a good person to start with, then proceed. One plan suggests the following steps:

1. Decide on a time for an organizational meeting and invite a local official, or some other knowledgeable person, to address the group on the pornography problem. Invite the city or county attorney, a police official, the postmaster, or some other official who has a genuine interest in curbing pornography.

2. Give careful attention to planning this initial meeting. The pastor can announce and support it. Promote it in the church bulletin and newsletter. Give special invitations to lawyers, politicians, businessmen, and school and police officials who are sympathetic. Utilize their wisdom and experience. Young people and parents may also be invited.

3. During the first part of the program, the speaker or speakers can present the problem and offer suggestions for action. Use the remaining part of the meeting for organization.

4. The type and degree of organization and action depends upon the nature of local problems and the interest in overcoming them. Elected officers could include a chairman, vice-chairman, secretary, and treasurer. Only a permanent chairman may be wanted.

5. Lead the group to set up subcommittees to undertake action to report back to the entire group.

(1) Committee on Markets and Bookstores

This committee has to organize itself to make periodical inspections of the places where books are sold such as newstands, magazine and book racks in local stores. When conducting surveys it's best for two or three persons to go together. If the committee finds obscene materials they may make a courteous objection to the manager, and if there is no response meet together to decide on a plan of action.

(2) Movie Committee

Set up a group, keep the movies under surveillance. Watch the newspaper ads. Keep your ear to the ground for reports of pictures that are presently being screened in your area.

Some cities have a "dial-a-movie" service which gives the rating of current movies: "G, PG, R, X." Other cities have a local classification board which rates those movies unfit for those under sixteen and have city ordinances, so far considered constitutional, backing up the rating regulations.

In many cities the newspapers refuse to accept advertisements for X-rated movies. This might be a possible line of action to minimize the influence of these movies.

Don't overlook the possibility of legal action. Consult the later section of this chapter on "Utilizing Your Legal Avenues."

(3) Television Monitoring Committee

As television is probably the most important single aspect of the media this whole enterprise should be organized very carefully.

(a) The committee needs to have at least four members each of whom will be assigned to a major network or public broadcasting service. In cities of less than four channels, the committee should consist of one person for each channel.

(b) Each of these members can have a subcommittee to work with. He should enlist five people to help him.

(c) Each member of the Monitor Committee should select one evening during the week, and watch every program between 7:00 or 7:30 and 11:00 p.m. He should write a brief report on every program he believes objectionable, and every one he thinks good, on his assigned network or channel.

(d) Reports should be concise. They should contain: date and day (e.g. Tuesday, November 21); time (8:30 p.m.); channel number, call letters and network; name of program; type of program (drama, variety, situation comedy); brief comments (suggestive situations, vulgarity, offensive theme, distorted sense of values; or positive comments in the case of praise-worthy programs).

(e) Chairmen should compile and condense reports, voice objections or praise in short, covering note, and send to the TV network involved, the local channel involved, the sponsors.

(4) Speakers Bureau

Organize available manpower so you can send speakers out to churches, schools, and service clubs to educate people about the local problems of pornography. P.T.A.'s often provide excellent opportunities, and many of them are hungry for program personalities.

There are two specialized organizations to help you in your task and will assist in setting up groups to cope with this menace. They are:

Morality in Media
487 Park Avenue
New York, New York 10022

Citizens For Decent Literature, Inc.
5670 Wilshire Boulevard
Los Angeles, California 90036

Both of these groups have had wide experience. They were founded by dissenting members of the President's Commission on Obscenity and Pornography and are anxious to help.

Be subtle in your approach—beware of demonstrations. You may give the pornographers the publicity they are seeking.

Always remember the word of former Postmaster General Blount, "The deciding factor is going to be the American public. If the people decide against pornography, we can do away with it."

Hit Them in the Cash Register

What is the basic motivation of the producers and sellers of pornography?

Love of art?

Concern about freedom of speech?

Convictions concerning artistic expression?

No, none of these.

The main motivation is financial.

As a believer in the free enterprise system, and one who dreads the lethargy that falls on a noncompetitive way of life, I have some uneasy moments as I survey the world of literature and art and see the power of money to corrupt both the art forms, causing writers and artists to capitulate to economic pressure and prostitute their talents before mammon. Pornography shows us the seamiest of capitalistic enterprise.

A recent interview of a photographer producing pictures for *Playboy* magazine turned up some significant aspects of the financial and motivational side of things. This photographer described his experience in going into a community, with his wife, ostensibly to make sure of an appearance of decency and respectability, and asking girls to model for pictures.

The approach uses a bait and switch technique. He begins by asking his subjects to model in their clothes, then starts the process of selling them on the artistic merits of *Playboy* magazine. The next step is to suggest they would like to do some pictures in the nude.

The greatest pressure, however, is financial. For these simple modeling chores the girls are paid $100-$150, but like the carrot before the donkey's nose is held out the possibility of being featured in the centerfold of *Playboy* as the "Playmate of the Month." If they are selected for this privileged position they receive $5,000, and extra fees probably push it to $6,000.

Put yourself in this girl's situation. Here is an opportunity for one chore of modeling that may pay her as much as she would be able to earn in a year of work. The temptation is overwhelming.

The same applies to writing. Consider the rates of pay for struggling writers, then look at what the pornographer is willing to give. Writing articles for magazines is a highly competitive business. Some magazines pay two and a half cents a word and others may go as high as ten cents a word. Suppose a writer pens a 5000 word article. At the ten cent rate, $500. Contrast that with *Playboy* magazine which for the same piece of writing if it is used as a lead article, will pay $3000. It is easy to see how a struggling writer would be tremendously attracted to these high rates of pay.

This financial consideration gives us a clue to one very effective tactic in combating the evil. The man who made the product, the middle man who distributed it, and the retailer who sells it or displays it all have in mind making a fast buck. Cut away the profits of these men and you have dealt them a deadly blow.

Take a stand. Refuse to attend movies that are off-color and tell the manager why you are staying away. Let him know that you are going to start a whispering campaign among your friends, urging them to pass up his theater. When he exhibits good quality movies encourage your friends to attend. Let him know it pays to exhibit family–type movies. If they contain objectionable material, tell the manager you'll trade somewhere else and why you are doing it. Moreover, let him know that you are going to tell the people at your church or your civic organization and urge them not to shop in his establishment. In a free enterprise system the customer's dollar speaks. Devise ways to cut off the money and you'll have a potent weapon against the peddler of filth.

Enlist the Women

At the head of all the objectionable features of pornography stands its attitude towards women who are exploited as sex objects, and depicted in the most degrading manner to provide masculine sexual stimulation.

In a day when women are conscious as never before of the discrimination against them, they should be one of the first groups to which we turn in mobilizing our forces against the mercenaries of smut.

The shrill voice of the angry woman sounded out in Madison Avenue, the symbol of America's fabulous advertising profession, as the speaker, a member of Women's Lib spoke out what many an outraged woman may have been thinking for a long time, "Sexists American advertising pigs are free woman's greatest enemy."

These demonstrators—women with a cause—were out to level their attack at the policies of advertisers who use women's bodies as a means of selling a whole raft of products.

Personally I am the old-fashioned type and I like a woman who marries, settles down, and becomes a capable wife, mother and housekeeper but I must confess there is something about many of these women that appeals to me. I feel they've had a dirty deal in the way that men have portrayed them as only being of value in terms of their sexuality.

Not all these women are dumpy little housewives, who spend their days locked up in their homes, without any real knowledge of what is going on in the artistic world. Mrs. Beverly Walker, a film producer herself, spoke out about the movie, *A Clockwork Orange,* showing that the film producer had distorted the original book to make the story more sexually titillating and she charged, "The film flaunts an attitude that is ugly, lewd and brutal toward the female human being. All the women are portrayed as caricatures; the violence committed upon them is treated comically; the most startling aspects of the decor relate to the female form."

Then with the indignation reserved for a thoroughly aroused woman Mrs. Walker recalled the way the Italian Anti-Defamation League had persuaded the producer to delete the word "Mafia" from the *The Godfather.* She came up with a practical idea, "We should start to think in terms of economic boycotts of films in which women are exploited mercilessly for the box-office dollar."

When Mrs. Walter Magee of Cleveland became the leader of the Central Federation of Women's Clubs she called upon the

clubs to join, "in a great sweeping nationwide crusade to rees-
tablish the meaning of the American home; to reaffirm the bas-
ics of the good life . . . honesty, forthrightness, decency,
peacefulness, respect for others . . . until our voice is heard
and heeded by those responsible for the current rash of violence, crime and lurid sex in our entertainment media." Members were asked to sign a statement or commitment—and
12,500 did so—voicing their concern with the rampant pornography in our society today.

As a result of this campaign within these organizations anti-
pornography laws were passed in Texas and Indiana. And the
advertising and exhibition of X-rated films were halted in many
communities.

There is no telling what a thoroughly aroused woman can do
in this situation. Get before the women's groups—P.T.A.,
Women's Clubs, Garden Clubs, Literary Clubs, Junior
Women's Clubs. Most of these women are mothers and grand-
mothers and gravely concerned about their children and grand-
children.

Emphasize the Consumer Angle

When like a band of vigilantes from a western movie, Ralph
Nader gathered together a group of young enthusiasts who
were quickly dubbed "Nader's Raiders, they gave consumerism a new lease on life and a glamour hitherto unknown.

Prodded by a rash of groups like this, the federal government has made some movies to help the general public make
good choices when spending their hard-earned dollars. Federal
Trade Commission has become increasingly aggressive in monitoring advertising and statements being made on behalf of various products; insisting that companies document their claims.
The tobacco industry has been forced to label its products with
a caution that, "The surgeon general has determined that cigarette smoking is dangerous to your health." And in some instances this government body has compelled companies to run
corrective advertisements pointing out the misinformation in
previous ads.

How about the pornographers?

Apparently the peddlers of smut live a charmed existence
and advertise products to build female busts, enlarge male genitals and make a series of improbable claims that are character-

istic of the con man. False information abounds on every hand. So-called educational materials, many of them allegedly prepared to help married couples make better sexual adjustment in marriage, and under the names of authors with Ph.D.'s appended, are a travesty of the educational process. These materials are packed full of factual errors and give a completely false idea of sexuality in the name of education.

Truth in advertising?

Consumer organizations have long been pushing the government to do something about products that may hurt people. So campaigns have been carried on against toys that splinter, or may injure, or materials that can easily catch fire and burn. What of the instrument for increasing masculine phallic size and capable of causing life-long impotency, and the dildos that could easily damage delicate female tissues, or whips and torture instruments for use by the artists of sadomasochism? Should not something be done about these?

And how about excessive profits? Cheaply produced materials are encased in cellopane so that they cannot be examined before purchasing and outrageously priced. Gullible young people come along and fork out their money. Isn't someone concerned about the people who are exploiting them?

The city of New York has led out in responding to the demands of the Consumer Affairs Department. It is headed by Bess Myerson of Miss America and T.V. fame, who had done yeoman service in insisting on truth in advertising but seems to have her hands tied in one area.

Writing in a series titled *Hell's Bedroom,* a reporter from a New York magazine, told about an interview with inspector Peterson of the New York Police Department. This officer made an evaluation of Miss Myerson's activities, "Bess Myerson is a sharp piece of work. But she's chasing roaches. Everybody's against roaches—what about the robbery cartel running these massage parlors?

Investigations revealed that the Department of Consumer Affairs had power, in the words of this reporter, ". . . to suspend and revoke licenses and to bring injunctive proceedings. In fact, it had more power than all the other city agencies *combined* over all of these establishments, *with the exception of massage parlors.*"[4]

The Department can busy itself with the cockroach problem,

check up to make sure of the weight of the vegetables purchased by the housewife, but when it comes to dealing with the exploitation of human sexuality not a thing can be done.

Pornographers stand preeminently as the parasites living off the gullible members of the general public, and if consumerism is to have any meaning, some voice must be raised in protest against the way naive people are being gypped by the smut merchants.

Utilize Legal Avenues

The pornographers are blatantly breaking the law with the hope that by clever legal moves they will be able to avoid its penalties. As law abiding citizens we must do everything we can to facilitate the enforcement of existing laws and the strengthening of weak laws that have been circumvented by these smut merchants.

Experts in the field say the most important and effective action is to report violations of community standards to the people responsible for enforcing the law. A citizen who has a complaint should direct it to the police, the prosecutor, city or county officials or to all of them combined.

The Attorneys of Citizens for Decent Literature have designed a form letter to be used in making a complaint.

> *To Prosecutor:*
>
> *In formal written complaint I bring to your attention what appears to be a violation of the state obscenity statute.*
>
> [Here list the publication by title, publisher, etc., or the motion picture title and the store or theater address, etc.]
>
> *I ask that you investigate this matter. If in your judgment the matter is in violation of the obscenity statute, I urge you to take the steps necessary to enforce the law.*
>
> _____
>   *Signature*

This type of complaint must be investigated and the fact that law enforcement officials must act on the complaint may serve as a deterrent to would-be violators.

Gaps in the Foundation?

"...IT IS FROM WITHIN, OUT OF THE HEARTS OF MEN THAT THERE COMES (ALL KINDS OF) EVIL..!!" — MARK 7:21 (20TH CENTURY N.T.)

If you receive pornography through the mail, there are several ways to respond.

One way is to merely reseal the envelope and mark it "Postal Inspector" across the front in large letters, then drop it into the mailbox.

Another legal avenue is to place a note in the package stating, "I believe this material may have been mailed in violation of the law, and I wish to request that you investigate the legality of the mailing."

Pack it up and mail the whole package to:

Law Department
U. S. Postal Service
Washington, D. C. 20560

Informed sources say this procedure has touched off many investigations that have resulted in federal prosecutions and convictions.

The tactic of the pornographer is to send his materials at the first class rate which means it cannot be intercepted as it comes through the mails. Consequently the Post Office must depend on patrons to report the matter before they can take action. When you request the intervention of the Postal authorities they are able to determine if legal action can be initiated.

You should also take advantage of a legal process that is open to citizens to help stop the flow of pornography. Under law 39 U. S. Code 3010 you can obtain form 2201 from the Post Office. Fill out this form with your name and address and the names of your children under 19 years of age. Your name will then be placed on Reference List which is available to mailers and if after you have been on the list for 30 days, you receive a sexually oriented advertisement, you should open the envelope then write on the outside, "I received this item May 9, 1972, signed John H. Doe," and take it to the Post Office.

Taking any or all of these actions means that you have struck a blow for democracy, it gives an indication to anyone who inquires, from Congress on down, that there are many citizens concerned about what comes through the mails and encourages the legislators to pass laws that will be a help in the battle against pornography. Most important of all, the prosecutor is able to utilize the information that a great number of citizens complained, to strengthen his case.

There are several sources for legal assistance. Citizens for Decent Literature offers the following services:

1. *RESEARCH MATERIALS—CDL maintains a complete library of all case law and briefs filed in obscenity cases. This extensive research library is available for use by prosecutors upon request and can greatly simplify the preparation of obscenity prosecutions.*

2. SEMINARS—CDL conducts seminars for prosecutors, judges, and law enforcement personnel to instruct them in new applications of existing criminal and civil law and to explain new developments in investigative techniques for evidence gathering for obscenity prosecutions. Seminars have been conducted for the National Association of District Attorneys, for prosecutive staffs in specific jurisdictions, as well as for judges and law enforcement agencies.

3. CDL—"FRIEND OF THE COURT"—CDL files Amicus Curiae briefs to support the prosecutor's position in obscenity cases at all levels of jurisdiction—including those before the United States Supreme Court.

4. DIRECT ASSISTANCE—CDL attorneys have been retained on a contract basis by civic officials to assist in setting up effective programs of obscenity law enforcement and prosecution.

5. CONSULTATION—CDL attorneys are available for consultation, suggestions or advice upon request from concerned citizens, government officials, law enforcement or prosecutive agencies.

The address of this organization is:

Citizens for Decent Literature, Inc.
5670 Wilshire Boulevard—Suite 1670
Los Angeles, California 90036

If your local prosecutor is having some difficulties in preparing his case, he can get assistance from either the legal section of Citizens for Decent Literature or a specially federally funded center:

National Legal Data Center
on the Law of Obscenity
California Lutheran College
3239 Regent Avenue
Thousand Oaks, California 91360

You must continue to press for effective laws at three levels.
Local Laws. Become familiar with the local laws concerning pornography. Enlist the help of a knowledgeable attorney and if the laws need strengthening, work towards that end. Keep the pressure on by writing letters and making personal contacts with members of the city council. Attend the city council meetings and commend the police for all they do and voice your concern about the situations that develop. Let the law enforce-

ment officers know of your interest and present them with evidence of violations of the law which you encounter.

State Laws. Take an interest in your state legislature. When candidates seek your vote, try to get a commitment from him that he will work for better state laws for controlling pornography. Remember the trend that seems to be towards state and local control. This will make the state legislature significantly more important in the future.

Federal Laws. We must have more effective national laws to control pornography. There are many pressures on congressmen, and the smut lobbyists have enlisted help from unlikely sources like the American Civil Liberties Union. Because of this you and your friends must add your voices to the forces on the side of decency. Write letters to national publications that will give them a wide readership. Let plans for new legislation be widely known.

Many years ago the perceptive Archbishop Temple observed, "To say that you cannot make folk good by Act of Parliament is to utter a dangerous half-truth. You can by Act of Parliament supply conditions which facilitate the growth of moral goodness and remove conditions which obstruct it." Let us continually stand at the alert to make sure that our lawmakers are aware of their responsibility to create a climate which facilitates morality and a concern for our fellow men.

As good citizens the law stands as our first defense against pornography.

Most people have heard the story of the Arab who lay resting in his tent and looked up to see a camel's head pushed in through the entrance flap.

Comfortably settled and at rest the tent owner did nothing to dislodge the interloper. Then in came a neck followed shortly afterwards by two front legs. Still no movement from the man—the camel walked right on in.

The tent owner by now had a conviction this had gone far enough and from his cramped corner he protested, "There isn't enough room for both of us in here."

The camel's response, "Well, get out."

Pornography is like this.

A resident of Copenhagen, Denmark, recently told a story strangely reminiscent of the camel in the tent theme.

In the discussion which preceded the Danish move to re-

IT GOT SO HE LIKED THE WALLOW

move the restrictions on pornography, the major argument from the liberal forces was that once pornography became freely available it would be "desensationalized," i.e. interest would wane and the whole trade eventually disappear.

The first move involved changing the law to allow free literary expression. Pictorial pornography was to remain under the strictures of the law.

Once written pornography became freely available for distribution, a new demand came for a similar freedom for visual material. The Minister of Justice then announced he planned to present Parliament with a bill removing restrictions on illustrated pornography. In an interview the minister made it clear that despite the freedom to allow distribution of illustrated material, no obscene matter would be displayed in public places and people to whom it was distasteful would not be confronted by it.

This reassurance meant the Minister of Justice was promising more than he could deliver. One resident tells how 60 pornography shops opened in an area in which he lived and, "Oversized signboards caught the eyes, loud speakers with bedroom scenes proclaimed that here was the real thing."

As the night the day followed new developments. A demand grew for flesh and blood shows in clubs for which any one could get a membership. A resident relates their nature, "The live show clubs show striptease, masturbation, go-go dancing, lesbian love, and orgies of sexual intercourse. Topless hostesses will dance with visitors, give intimate massage, and see to it that the guests feel relaxed and well disposed both during and after the show."

Is it any wonder that one disgusted Dane protested that his beloved country, instead of being a democracy, has become a *pornocracy*.

This is exactly the danger which we face in America today. The demands begin on a high level citing such things as freedom of artistic expression, first amendment guarantees, and a bit at a time the menace creeps in, and we who are so proud of being the "land of the free" face the very real danger of becoming a pornocracy.

The camel in the tent story may provide us with a clue to the final answer to pornography's threat. What if the Arab had so occupied his residence that there was no room for the beast to enter?

In the ultimate, pornography finds a hospitable welcome in spiritually barren spots.

When Lord Longford, the British peer, instigated the British investigation into the problems of pornography many people wondered why he should become involved in such a difficult undertaking. One reason was his visit to a London theater where he was repelled by a performance of "Oh Calcutta!" A second and perhaps overriding motivation was spelled out in the introduction to *The Longford Report* where the peer says, "In fact I was 65 years old before, as far as I can remember, the word pornography ever passed my lips in public. I regard concern about pornography as simply one corner, though a vital and much neglected corner, of a Christian approach to our fellow humans."[5]

In the same way that historically paganism with its perverse sexual practices, was overwhelmed by what one historian calls, "the cleansing tide of Christian ethics," so in our day we need a great revival of spiritual ideals that will subdue the pornographic thrust.

Notes

CHAPTER ONE

1. The end of 1972 brought the end of one of the most successful and prestigious magazines as *Life* published its last issue.

Bob Warden lamented the passing of *Life* in terms of its contribution to the culture of our society.

"Where else is there a mass magazine with the money and enterprise to commission such features as 'King's Story,' by Edward, Duke of Windsor?

"Where else, in the same issue, will you get photo essays on Helen Hayes, a Columbia River Basin dam, and the life of a black widow spider, including the devouring of her mate in the love-making process?

"Who will print a distinguished novel, as *Life* did Hemingway's *The Old Man and the Sea* before the book comes out?

"Who will introduce us to the works of great American painters before they become great, as *Life* introduced us to Edward Hopper, Charles Burchfield, Paul Sample, and Jackson Pollack?

"Where will we get a spread on Andy Warhol or Claes Olderburg from the same magazine that shows us Michaelangelo's 'Last Judgment' and the ceiling of the Sistine Chapel?

"Who will publish the memoirs of the future Winston Churchills, Harry Trumans, Douglas MacArthurs and Charles de Gaulles?

"Where else could you see anything like the 18-page spread of Swedish photographer Lennart Nilsson's 'Drama of Life Before Birth,' including a color picture stretched across two pages of a laboratory simulation of 200 million sperm swimming up the Fallopian tube?

"Would any other popular magazine print the 'Lost Notebooks of Leonardo Da Vinci,' turned up in 1967 by a professor in the Madrid library where they had been miscatalogued a century earlier?

"That's what *Life* was about."

Let the reader ponder this lament and recollect another of Warden's statements, " . . . about 160 other magazines . . . failed or were merged into oblivion in the last decade."

Columnist Jim Bishop recently noted (Dallas Times Herald, April 22, 1972), "Once upon a long ago a boy would appear at your front door offering four or six magazines at cut rate subscription prices. He's gone. He's grown up. His son prefers to read some cheap toilet paper sheet which tells him who is making it with whom, in addition to photographs."

He rather sadly adds, "People no longer want informative articles and good fiction, they want sex."

CHAPTER TWO

1. *Atlantic,* January 1972, p. 87.
2. *Atlantic,* January 1972, p. 88.
3. *Newsweek,* May 18, 1970, p. 75.
4. *McCalls,* October 1970, p. 140.
5. Hy Gardner, "Glad You Asked That," *Anderson (S.C.) Independent,* March 25, 1972, p. 2.
6. O. Hobart Mowrer, *The New Group Therapy* (Princeton: D. Van Nostrand Company, Inc., 1964), p. 184.
7. *McCalls,* October 1970, p. 140.
8. *Atlantic,* August, 1971, p. 24.

CHAPTER THREE

1. *Dallas Times Herald,* April 22, 1972.
2. Julia A. Sherman, "What Men Do Not Know About Women's Sexuality," *Medical Aspects of Human Sexuality, November 1972, p. 146.*
3. *Ibid.,* pp. 139-40.
4. Valerie sets out the details of her early sex life; how she lost her virginity, pregnancy, an illegal abortion. So go the scenes that lead the reader to conclude that if a wider experience of every variety of sexual experience, including fellatio, cunnilingus, sadomasochistic practices is essential for a sexual "therapist," this girl had the broadest-based training possible. The descriptions of the actual therapy sessions themselves are excuses for reviewing the clients past sexual experiences and then describing the "therapist's" effort to revive this male's sexual interest. In the manner of all pornography, erotic scenes are carefully timed in their presentation and minutely detailed to provide the greatest aphrodisiacal effect.

Although her abilities as a sex therapist might be suspect, no one can question the capacity of either Valerie X, or her collaborator, to use eroticising techniques when recounting her alleged experiences.

CHAPTER FOUR

1. Richard S. Randall, "Classification by the Motion Picture Industry," *Technical Report of the Commission on Obscenity and Pornography,* Volume V, U.S. Goverąment Printing Office, Washington, D.C., pp. 222-23.

2. "Motion Pictures," *Technical Report of the Commission on Obscenity and Pornography,* Volume III, U.S. Government Printing Office, Washington, D.C., p. 30.

3. *Ibid.,* p. 37.

4. Randall, Volume V, p. 259.

5. *Ibid.,* p. 263

It seems to be mighty strange in these days when the consumer protection movement is so strong that for every supermarket product to have its ingredients spelled out, along with a plain, easy-to-understand statement about the exact price of the product that is being purchased, advertisements which are to provide parents with guidance about the movie choice for their children should completely omit the one vital piece of information which they need.

Worse still is the "bait-and-switch" operation that has been the forte of the crooked salesman. We have already noted the use of trailers at movie houses so that someone who has gone to see a family type movie is suddenly subjected to a series of trailers for sex-saturated films that will be screened in the near future. To further the deception, the trailers come in two varieties: "hot" and "cool." If it is of the cool variety, it may give the impression that the coming attraction may not be too bad and encourage attendance.

6. "Abuse of Film Ratings," *New York Times,* April 27, 1972.

7. Randall, Volume V, p. 276.

8. *Ibid* 221

Despite the claim by the movie makers that they are producing "adult movies" in response to the demands of their mature audiences, surveys of people attending the screenings of their movies indicate the typical movie-goer is an older adolescent or a young adult. While the mature will occasionally bestir himself to attend a showing of *Fiddler on the Roof,* by and large, these mature adults, for whom the producers have been working so hard in making their movies, view the finished product infrequently, or not at all.

As our examination of the rating system has shown, the theater owners have neither advertised their ratings nor policed their admissions with any real measure of responsibility. They actually take a certain unctious pride in pushing responsibility of the children's film fare back on the parents. This makes it all the more important that parents should know what is being shown in the local theater.

No one who observes the present movie scene can doubt that the job to block censorship was remarkably well done and the much vaunted function of ratings to inform parents has been a complete fizzle. One only has to look at the way ratings have changed with convenient flexibility. Add to this the manner in which the advertisements have abused the presentation of ratings and the sorry way the theaters have acted in admitting people—in the majority of cases without restriction.

It all adds up to the fact that parents don't know what rating the movies have and theaters won't really restrict admissions. Moreover, the rating system does not present any opinion of the content or the legality of film productions as far as adults are concerned. It only provides opinions as to whether the film is suitable for children under 17.

Why not?

We have truth in labeling laws for other products. Doesn't the customer have a right to know what he is spending his money on? What if supermarkets insisted that customers pay for groceries before they had a chance to know what they were buying? How about the X-rated material exhibited as a sneak preview on an alleged trailer telling of coming attractions?

In a country that breaks up monopolies and seeks to concern itself with the rights and privileges of the common man we have a right to expect some type of control over the activities of people who wield such an influence on the minds of men and women. While we are being reminded of the rights of the movie producers, we had better give a thought to the rights of his customers.

9. Victor B. Cline, "An Assessment of Behavior Norms Modeled in Current Motion Picture Screenplays," Unpublished Paper, p. 9.

10. *Ibid.*, p. 12.

11. Hollis Allpert and Arthur Knight, "Sex in Cinema," *Playboy,* (November 1970), p. 219.

12. *Sexology,* March 1971.

13. Randall, Volume III, p. 60.

14. Cline, p. 14.

15. *Dallas Morning News,* December 6, 1972.

16. *Ibid.*

CHAPTER FIVE

1. Herbert A. Otto, "Communes The Alternative Life Style," *The Saturday Review,* April 24, 1971, p. 17.

2. Bell, *Sexual Behavior,* May 1971.

3. *Ibid.*, p. 68.

4. *Ibid.*, p. 156.

5. *Human Sexuality,* May 1971, p. 73.

CHAPTER SIX

1. All the evidence indicates that lesbians are probably less promiscuous than their masculine counterparts, and the propaganda drive seeks to make capital out of this and portray two women setting up beautiful, long-lasting relationships.

However, this very factor may bring complications that seem to beset lesbian relationships. A voluntary association of two people who have no legal commitment to each other is frequently beset by deep and hostile jealousies.

One authority in the field states the situation very concisely. "Gaining control of the partner, or gaining the assurance of being benevolently controlled by the partner, is an almost ever present feature of the lesbian relationship. The unusual amount of hostility and even physical violence found in so many of these liaisons may be related to this struggle. One needs to control and possess, or to be controlled and possessed, and that gnawing need is often frustrated—by infidelity, rejection, or simple refusal. The result is often a seemingly irrational, uncontrollable and infantile rage." (Fred Belliveau and Lin Richter, *Understanding Human Sexual Inadequacy* (New York: Bantam Books, 1970), pp. 54-55.

2. Barry M. Dank, *Sexual Behavior,* March, 1972, p. 5.

3. Evidence of this attitude is seen in some of the publications which come from various parts of the country. Their titles include *Nekids, Naked Boyhood, Young Boys and Sex Review, 2000 Boys, Boy Studies, Nudist Youth, Playtime Teens,* and consist mainly of photographs of boys, many of them juveniles. One publication has a whole series of pictures of boys eight to ten years old showing them naked, picturing phallus or buttocks. These magazines are usually a regular part of the pornography shelves. Defenders of pornography are plainly frustrated when trying to justify their existence.

4. Dallas City Attorney, N. Alex Bickley, personal communication.

5. *Time,* June 5, 1972, *Dallas Times Herald,* May 29, 1972.

6. *Sexual Behavior,* November 1971, p. 17.

7. John W. Drakeford, *Forbidden Love* (Waco: Word, Inc., 1971), p. 135.

8. Daniel Cappon, *Toward an Understanding of Homosexuality* (Englewood Cliffs, N.J.: Prentice Hall Inc., 1965), pp. 115, 126.

9. U.P.I. Release, October 2, 1972.

CHAPTER SEVEN

1. *Pix,* Vol. 4, #3, September 1971, p. 52.

2. In true discount house fashion the establishments are replete with a catalog which has an introductory speel, "If in case of an accident, injury or loss of the male member, sex relations are impossible, true-to-nature artificial members made of latex are indispensible. With their help, the man enables his partner to practice the function essential to her happiness. These aids are recommended by psychologists and doctors for cases of functional impotence."

If, as this blatant piece of hypocrisy maintains, the Sex Supermarkets exist to help men who have been multilated, one can only conclude that some devastating destruction hitherto unknown has been perpetrated on the male population. As with so much of the porno trade, the whole statement is a fiction to cover up the true intent of their activities and the claim that such gadgets help functional impotence is another indication of the imaginative capacity of public relations men and advertising agencies. We will later on see that major studies have indicated that this preoccupation with sexual performance may itself be a major factor in causing such impotence, and is consequently no cure.

One advertisement comes up with an element of truth when it suggests that the bachelor can look after his sexual needs and this will enable him, " . . . to dispense with women altogether."

So it came to pass that the "do it yourself" literature that has burgeoned to help the hobbyist build a boat, paint by numbers, enlarge the den, or antique the furniture has been added a new angle—"do it yourself" sex. Of course sex is an experience that normally involves two people, and about the only sexual activity that readily lends itself to "do it yourself" techniques, is autoeroticism, so masturbation has attained a new prominence in the world of eroticism.

3. Irving Kristol, "Pornography, Obscenity and the Case for Censorship," *New York Times,* March 28, 1971, p. 112.

4. William H. Masters and Virginia E. Johnson, "Advice to Young Women," *Redbook,* January, 1972, p. 124.

5. Sex is the unifying factor in marriage. If some type of sexual activity disrupts the marriage it may be necessary to take a second look at that particular practice.

In one counseling center, it has been frequently reported that in problems of adjustment a closer investigation will often reveal that one partner or the other, while denying sexual access to a spouse, will be finding personal sexual satisfaction by masturbation. Such an attitude can hardly by any stretch of the imagination be referred to as natural, healthy, and beneficial.

O. Hobart Mowrer, speaking not as an evangelical Christian but as a psychologist, tells about a counselee who confessed to post-marital masturbation in these words: "As I now see the situation, masturbation on the part of a husband is likely to be damaging to the marriage relationship primarily because it keeps him from being sufficiently dependent upon his wife. He does not need to work at preserving deeply satisfying personal relations with her. If she withdraws from him sexually or ceases to be alluring to him, he no longer needs her. He, so to say, can provide a 'vigina' himself and, in fantasy, attach it to any woman in the world. In this type of withdrawal, not only is the man depriving himself of the maturing effect that comes from having to 'get along' with one's wife, he is also inflicting a wrong upon her in denying her her sexual rights and perhaps encouraging her to fall into similarly solitary and demoralizing practices. (Unpublished paper).

Within the marriage bond the activity may be a gesture of defiance, an affront, a symbolic cutting off from one's mate.

In this situation it is not good.

One of the most liberal spokesmen for sexual freedom is R. E. L.

Masters. In the introduction to his book, *Sexual Self-Stimulation,* he puts forth a case for consideration of masturbation as a different kind of sexual pleasure rather than inferior. Then he goes on to say, "Taking a long range perspective, however, it ought to be recognized that the elimination of self-stimulation is desirable." (R.E.L. Masters, *Sexual Self-Stimulation,* Los Angeles: Sherbourne Press, Inc., 1967, p. 13.)

CHAPTER EIGHT

1. *The Report of the Commission on Obscenity and Pornography,* Bantam Books Edition, p. 462.

Each of these "technical reports" contains a foreword stating with what satisfaction the Commission makes the reports available and goes on to invite "critical examination and appraisal of these reports." But even as the interested reader finds himself commending the open-minded attitude of the Commission he discovers one peculiarity. On the title page of each volume is the statement, "This technical report has not been reviewed or approved by the full commission."

One immediate question comes to mind—"If this is an account of the basic research upon which the Commission based its findings and if they want the general public to read and appraise these reports, how come the members of the Commission have not read the reports themselves?" With that question in mind the reader has stumbled upon one of the strangest aspects of this highly controversial commission.

Several Commission members claim this inscription inviting the public to examine the reports the members themselves have not "reviewed or approved," typified the relationship of the Commission to the investigation they were supposed to be engaged in. What actually happened was that a hand-picked professional staff undertook the research contracting with a number of people or groups of researchers to perform a series of studies, the results of which were prepared by the professional staff, and the completed job was presented to the Commission for its rubber stamp. Three Commissioners claimed that when they requested permission to *examine* certain of the basic technical research reports of investigations, carried out on behalf of the Commission, they were circumvented and only finally saw the materials, " . . . after repeated dogged requests."

The general public knew virtually nothing of what was going on in this enterprise. The Commissioners claimed they were following the mandate of Congress, to do a thorough investigation of the subject before coming up with their recommendations. Despite the fact that the Chairman was a member of the American Civil Liberties Union, and believed people had a right to know what was going on in government, and should have free and open access to information, when it came to news about the proceedings of the Commission, it had been decided only one spokesman should give any reports about its activities. The rest of the members were muzzled.

Americans have not had the happiest experiences with presidential commissions.

One member of the Commission blames the structure, "So-called Presidential Commissions do not work. They never will. Such Commissions, in my opinion, are not a valid part of the American political system. The structure of the Commission on Obscenity and Pornography was similar to that of other Commissions. This Commission was not responsible to anyone, either to the President who appointed it, the Congress which created it, or to the people who the Congress represented." (Rossell Kirk, *Manchester Union Leader,* March 14, 1972, p. 1)

Others have been concerned about the leadership, "Nearly all those presidential commissions—on pornography, or campus disorders and so forth—have been worthless or baneful and one reason for the failure of such presidential commissions has been the incompetence of the gentlemen appointed to head them."

While his competence in his field was never under question, the Chairman of the Commission on Obscenity and Pornography became the center of controversy and this in a large measure because of his affiliation with the American Civil Liberties Union.

For many years the A.C.L.U. has taken the position that any form of censorship is undesirable, and that "obscenity as much as any other form of speech or press is entitled to the protection of the First Amendment." When legislation was first introduced with the aim of setting up the Commission on Obscenity and Pornography, the A.C.L.U. vigorously opposed the idea. As it became apparent the Commission would be established, the A.C.L.U. changed its tune, and the Director of the Washington Office of the organization, testified before the House Sub-Committee on Education and Labor, and called for "scientific studies" strongly emphasizing the point that *the public* and private groups should not be involved in the activities of the Commission.

Despite the declaration of the enabling legislation that the chairman would be elected by the Commission, a news release from the White House dated January 2, 1968, announced the appointment of William B. Lockhart to that position. Coincidentally, an influential personality in the White House at this time was Mr. Jack Valenti, who later, as spokesman of the movie industry, was to introduce the "flexible" rating system, and bragged that this system had been responsible for preventing state and local boards from imposing government censorship on films.

The announcement of the chairman failed to note that Public Law 90-100, which created the Commission, stated, "Congress finds that the traffic in obscenity and pornography is a matter of national concern," but Mr. Lockhart, the new chairman, had co-authored a legal article presenting a different perspective as he concluded, " . . . the evils that are often supposed to result from obscenity are either not really evils or do they pose such a clear and present danger to substantial social interests." An impartial observer might well have wondered how this chairman reconciled these two opposing perspectives.

To further compound the situation the chairman insisted on the appointment of another member of A.C.L.U. as the Commission's Chief Legal Counsel. Mr. Bender, the gentleman in question, attended the meetings of the Commission from the beginning, and one Commission member claims that Mr. Lockhart had stated unless Mr. Bender were appointed to the position of Chief Legal Counsel, he (Lockhart), would resign.

The eighteen members of the Commission were divided into four panels—the legal panel, the traffic panel, the effects panel, and the positive approaches panel. Each of these panels in turn assigned responsibilities to the permanent staff, who either did investigation themselves or contracted the work out to other researchers.

As some members of the Commission saw the situation this body had become a group of spectators at the best, or puppets at the worst. The professional staff took up the ball and ran with it. Meetings of the panels were planned by the professional staff who prepared the agendas for the gatherings. There were no by-laws, no parliamentary procedure for approval or amendment of the minutes of the meeting.

Fragmentation was also charged by the dissenters. They claimed the panels worked separately, and none knew what was happening in the other's meetings. The total group originally met every other month, but from October, 1969, to March, 1970, there were five months between meetings.

The mandate to the Commission in Public Law 90-100 contained two sections indicating the importance of the Commission consulting with a variety of representatives at federal, state, and local levels. These sections appeared to call for some types of public hearings, but the A.C.L.U. had taken a stand against such procedures, and coincidentally the Commission took the same attitude.

When two dissident Commissioners decided the time had come to take some action and held public hearings, the Commission refused to reimburse them for their expenses. Later, the Commission did conduct two public hearings of its own, but the dissenters claimed the action was taken in the hope of gaining public acceptance of the final majority report.

2. *Ibid.*, p. 65.

3. *U.S. News and World Report,* January 25, 1971, p. 68.

4. *The Report of the Commission on Obscenity and Pornography,* Bantam Books Edition, p. 467.

5. *Ibid.*

6. *Ibid.*, p. 169.
7. *Ibid.*, p. 463.
8. This was not an unreasonable request as it is accepted in the scientific world that experimental studies can be repeated in anticipation of reaching the same conclusions. Consequently a re-examination of the research plans and finding could only augur well for people committed to scientific research.

The Commission was not willing to do this, so Dr. Cline agreed to serve as an unpaid consultant to the minority members who dissented from the findings of the Commission and in this role undertook to make a thorough examination of the research.

Obviously the staff workers of the Commission were not impressed by Cline and showed a reluctance, strange for people who are scientific in their approach, to make available the statistics upon which they based their findings.

When Cline finally obtained these materials he applied his critical scientific eye to them and made some startling discoveries. His assessment was: "A careful review and study of the Commission majority report, their conclusions and recommendations, and the empirical research studies on which they were based, reveal a great number of serious flaws, omissions and grave shortcomings which make parts of the report suspect and to some extent lacking in credibility."

The interested reader should take some time to read the details of Cline's criticism as appended to the majority report in the context of the Hill Link minority statement.

As the celebrated English authority, Professor Eysenck, stated in a comment on the Commission's findings, "Anyone interested in these matters ought to read both sides (and the original ten volumes as well, if patience permits); they provide a wonderful example of one-sided reporting, biased selection of evidence, and failure to base conclusions on the evidence." (*Pornography—The Longford Report* (London: Coronet Books, 1972), p. 120.)

CHAPTER NINE

1. *The Report of the Commission on Obscenity and Pornography,* Bantam Books Edition, p. 485.
2. Eberhard and Phyllis Kromhausen, *Pornography and the Law* (New York: Ballantime Books, 1959), p. 263.
3. *Pornography—The Longford Report*, p. 122.
4. *Ibid.*, p. 123.
5. *Ibid.*, p. 125.
6. *Time*, November 6, 1972, p. 69.
7. *Pornography—The Longford Report*, p. 31.
8. *Time*, April 5, 1971, p. 64.

CHAPTER TEN

1. *The Report of the Commission on Obscenity and Pornography,*

Bantam Books Edition, p. 490.

2. *Ibid.,* p. 491.

3. *Time,* January 15, 1973, p. 46.

4. *Dallas Times Herald,* June 27, 1972.

5. Pete Hamil, *America,* June 12, 1971, p. 614.

6. Kuh, *Foolish Figleaves* (New York: The MacMillan Company, 1967), p. 273.

7. James A. Mitchener, "The Weapons We Need to Fight Pornography," *Readers Digest,* December, 1968, p. 129.

8. *Ibid.,* p. 130.

CHAPTER ELEVEN

1. Kinsey, Pomeroy, Martin, Gebhard, *Sexual Behavior in the Human Female* (Philadelphia: W. B. Saunders Company, 1953), p. 502-3.

2. Cosmopolitan, December 1972, p. 226.

3. Lester Velie, "The War on the American Family," *Readers Digest* (January, 1973), p. 109.

4. *Ibid.*

5. "Love Marquesan Style," *Human Sexuality,* September 1972, p. 55.

6. *Parade,* November 19, 1972.

7. The residents of Fort Worth, Texas, were understandably horrified by the news that a 23-year-old man had sexually mutilated and raped an 85-year-old woman.

Searching for the suspect, the police stumbled upon a lead when they apprehended a man carrying an attache case full of pornographic literature. He turned out to be their man.

What role did pornography play in this sex crime?

The Presidential Commission on Pornography and Obscenity came up with another of its incomprehensible conclusions when it speculated that sexual offenders frequently looked around for something to blame for their crime, and consequently their reports about the influence of pornography were a process of "scapegoating." The Commission concluded, "On the basis of the available data, however, it is not possible to conclude that erotic material is a significant cause of sex crime."

Despite this confident assertion, the evidence which we see on every hand will not allow us to casually dismiss the role of pornography in motivating sexual crimes.

From across the nation come a flood of reports telling the same story.

In California, a male youth, aged 20, attacked a twelve-year-old girl on her way home from school. The young man had a girlie magazine in his possession.

A gang of boys in Oklahoma ranging from 7 to 15 years old specialized in group sexual activities. They reported buying pornographic magazines in grocery and in drugstore newsstands and said that these gave them ideas for their way-out sexual activities.

A police officer, while patrolling in a park in California, came upon a boy performing an act of sodomy on another boy. The offender was using the center spread of *Playboy* magazine as a means of sexual stimulation.

Arrested for molesting a ten-year-old girl, a man in Georgia told the examining psychiatrist that he frequently bought books illustrated by "women wearing varying amounts of clothing and assuming suggestive positions."

8. Here are three front marquee advertisements for movies.

The One Big
  IF . .
you embarrass easily
you are not broad-minded
you cling to false modesty
you are not 18 (or over)

Our Presentations
Are **NOT** for You!

We show the **strongest adult action** movies in the city—couples welcome!

Star Adult Theater—X-Rated

ENTRANCE—**if** the naked human body offends you
Please DO NOT enter these doors—must be 18.

ADULT MOVIE—**Yes,** We're Open!
—**not** recommended for anyone with hangups!
Escorted ladies admitted Free—
ALL MOVIES RATED XXX

These are typical X-rated theater marquees in hundreds of cities.

The implication of these ads is that if you don't take in X-rated movies there's something wrong. Not having a need to view the pornographer's art you must be a juvenile, a naive goody-goody who was behind the door when virile, down-to-earth attributes were handed out.

9. Kinsey, p. 672.

10. Irving Kristol, "Pornography, Obscenity and the Case for Censorship," *New York Times Magazine,* March 28, 1973, p. 112.

11. *Foolish Figleaves,* p. 284.

CHAPTER TWELVE

1. *Playboy,* October 1970, p. 154.

2. *Pornography—The Longford Report,* p. 126.

3. *Playboy,* November 1972.

4. Gail Sheeny, "The Landlords of Hell's Bedroom," *The New York Magazine,* November 20, 1972, p. 72.

5. *Pornography—The Longford Report,* p. 14.